Indelible Memories

Of the incidents that created the person I am today

Carol J. Neumann

Willabay Press, LLC
Williams Bay, WI
2020

Although the author has attempted to ensure the accuracy and completeness of the information contained in this book, we assume no responsibility for errors, inaccuracies, omissions or any inconsistencies herein. Any slights of people or organizations are unintentional.

Table of Contents

Introduction

Indelible Memories is a book-length memoir composed of a series of short vignettes covering those moments in life when I gained important understandings about life as I observed what was going on around me. Some of the vignettes have been published separately in small literary journals.

The overall conflict in the book has to do with my deteriorating and lost relationship with my parents and my feeling of abandonment after the loss of my mother. They get resolved, mostly by my growing understanding of Dad and his ways and by the transfer of my allegiances to the wide world in general. But still, those feelings I had as a little girl persist even as I realize all I learned from them and how much I am like them now.

Dedicated to my family, my teachers and the friends I grew up with who helped me to grow into the person I am. And to the friends in the DuPage Writers Group and the Society of Children's Books Writers and Illustrators who have helped me so much with my writing.

**Me and Daddy by the rabbit hutch, Richie in the
background – 1947**

Bare Naked Beginnings

I opened my eyes and rubbed them with my hands. I could see the light coming in through the window between the bars of my crib. I rolled over and looked at the big bed across the room. My Mumma wasn't in it, so I cried for her. She didn't come so I sat up and called her.

"Mumma. Mumma."

But it was Daddy that entered the room, not Mumma. He was dressed in his overalls and had a special smile for me. He held his hands behind his back, laughing.

"Tut, tut, tut," he clucked his tongue. "Don't cry, Cookie. I have something for you."

Mumma ran into the room in a flowery dress and stood just behind him. She smiled at me and looked at Daddy.

"C'mon George, don't tease."

Daddy pulled his arm around and pushed something in my face. It was a dolly. I grabbed her with both hands and hugged her. She was darker than my other dollies and she had on a bright dress, the color of dandelions. I loved her right away.

"She's a n____r[1] doll," said Daddy.

"N____r doll," I thought about my dollies. Now I had Cutie, Susie Ann, and N____r Doll.

It was my first birthday. I didn't know it at the time. But I knew that I was Cookie and that Mumma and Daddy loved me, as did the other kids.

Daddy picked me up and carried me through the pantry. I noticed the cookie jar as we passed. It was my favorite part of the pantry. It had a big flower on the front.

"Cookie?" I asked.

"No, no. It's your birthday. We'll have cake."

"Cookie, cookie." I cried.

"Oh, give her one George. It's her birthday," said Mumma.

Daddy opened the jar and pulled one out. I grabbed it with both hands and sucked on it. It was sweet and made my mouth feel wet and happy.

"Cookie?" I held it up to give Mumma a bite.

Mumma nibbled the edge and said, "Tank-ou."

---

[1] Use of that racial slur was common in the 1940s. I don't think Daddy used it to offend.

I laughed and wiggled to get loose from Daddy. He carried me into the kitchen and put me down on the hard floor. I grabbed a chair and pulled myself up. I looked up at the big red pump.

"Wa-wa?"

Daddy pulled the long handle up and down until the water began to stream out of the pump. He filled my cup and handed it to me. The water was cool on my lips and my mouth felt good.

I could hear the sounds of the other kids outside and I wanted to go out, but Mumma grabbed me and lay me down to change my diaper. As soon as she had the diaper off, as she reached for the clean one, I got up and ran out the back door onto the porch.

"Cookie?" I could hear Mumma chasing after me. I scrambled down the porch steps and ran out onto the driveway. The big black car was parked in front of the garage. I ran around it and sat on the running board on the other side facing the barn. My bare butt felt warm from the hot car. I giggled in the sunshine, free and happy.

"Where's Cookie?" I could hear Mumma but I couldn't see her. I giggled some more. She found me, snatched me up and brought me back into the house.

"Big girls don't go outside bare naked," she said.

I wondered why.

The car where I sat on the running board

Supper was a big deal that night. My birthday cake was in the middle of the table. Everybody laughed over N____r Doll. "Just like Beulah," said my brother Jimmy. I had heard Beulah on the radio.

They didn't laugh like that about Susie Ann and Cutie.

My high chair was pushed up to the table by my plate with the birdie on it. I picked up my spoon and stuck it in the 'tatoes.

"Did you see Cookie outside bare naked?" asked Mumma.

"I did," said Chi-Chi. "She was sitting on the running board, hiding."

"Naughty girl," said my brother Ritchie.

"Tut, tut. She's just a baby," said Daddy.

4

I thought I was a big girl.

After supper, there was fire on the cake and singing and soon it was time to go to bed.

I lay in my crib with my girlie blanket and wondered about things. Then, I hugged Cutie and Susie Ann and N____r Doll and dreamed about running bare naked in the driveway, laughing.

It is the first day of my life that I remember, maybe because of things I didn't understand.

Whose Little Girl?

I was standing on the back seat of the black Chevy that morning with a box of crayons. I set the crayons on the shelf under the back window and pulled them out, one at a time. On tippy-toes, I reached up and made pretty wax circles on the glass. Red and blue and green and yellow – all the colors I loved made the window look prettier and prettier. Mumma would be happy to see my nice picture.

She wasn't. Instead, she was real mad when she found me. I got put down for an early nap. She and my big sister Lucy spend a lot of time scraping all the pretty colors off. I cried when I saw it. I had worked so hard, but I was a bad girl.

A couple of days later, something was really wrong. Mumma put a lot of my clothes in a bag and took me across the street to Myrtle and Ozzie's house. She said I was going to be Myrtle's little girl and I should be good. She was going to someplace called a hospital. Was it because I had been bad?

I tried to be good for Myrtle, but I sure missed Mumma and Daddy.

One day, Daddy picked me up at Myrtle's with Chi-Chi and Ritchie and we went to the hospital to see Mumma. We went down a long hallway with lots of doors. Mumma was lying on white sheets in a nightgown that I had never seen before. She showed me how it was open in the back. It looked pretty cold.

The hospital smelled funny, like when Mumma did Spring-cleaning. Next to Mumma's bed was a high table on wheels. It moved pretty fast if you pushed it. I guess I wasn't supposed to though, because Mumma yelled when I did. There was a glass on top of the table with a straw that could bend right over. As soon as I saw it, I wanted a drink of water.

"There's a fountain in the hallway," the nurse told us, so Ritchie and Chi-Chi took me into the hallway.

I couldn't reach, so Ritchie held me up there while Chi-Chi ran the water.

"Just put your mouth in the water and suck," said Chi-Chi.

I had never tried a drinking fountain before. The water went in my nose and eyes before I got my mouth in it. I sucked hard but not a drop of water went down my throat. I started to cry.

The nurse came out and saw our dilemma.

"I have just the thing," she said. She went and got me a glass of water with one of those "bendy" straws just like Mumma had.

You could bend it every which way and still get the water to go through. It was great. Ritchie and Chi-Chi wanted one too.

Mumma came home a few days later. Myrtle brought me to her. Mumma put her arms out for me. I wasn't sure what this meant. Was I still "Myrtle's little girl?" Or was I "Mumma's little girl" again? I was confused and cried. Mumma laughed, so I guessed it was ok.

I stayed with Mumma that night and everything was all right again, at least for a while.

7

Indelible Memories

My family talked about an operation with a big name. (It was a hysterectomy, but wasn't until I was middle-aged that I ever knew it was due to cancer). I was 2 ½ at the time, but I didn't know that.

Angel in a White Box

We still had the black Chevy with the running boards when it happened, whatever "it" was. No one told me.

It was the dead of winter when the snow banks were so high that I could ski right over the fence into the barnyard, only I shouldn't because the bull was out. No one told me that either. I was three and a half.

A hush came over the family. Mumma and Daddy packed us all in the car to go to the wake.

"What's a wake?"

"It's when someone dies, like great aunt Tillie," said my sister Chi-Chi who was almost seven.

"Then we wake them up?"

"No, of course not."

We drove way out in the country to Jerry and Marie's farmhouse. When we got there, we parked on the road and slipped and slid in our boots past lots of other cars, then over the driveway to the porch. Marie let us in. We piled our coats on the bed in the downstairs bedroom like we did for birthday parties, only I could tell this was sadder. Marie had tears in her eyes.

We went into the front room and there was a big white box, long and narrow, on top of a table. Everybody was praying around it: the ladies in their best dresses, smelling of flowery perfume; the men in suits, stinking of tobacco.

"What's in the box?"

"An angel."

"A real angel with wings?"

9

Indelible Memories

"I guess."
"Can I see it?"
"No, it's in heaven."
"Thought it was in the box."
Cyril, Phyllis, and Lois, all younger cousins, were playing on the floor, behind the table with the box. They sat on the wooden boards on the edge of the room, beyond the carpet. I joined them on the floor in my best red dress. I sat on my butt on the floor, with my knees bent on either side of me and my feet out sideways like three year olds do. We bounced a rubber ball with blue and yellow painted swirls. It went back and forth from Cyril to Phyllis to Lois to me. When somebody missed, they crawled under the table with the angel in the box to get it.

Cyril's brother David brought us frosted white cutout cookies. We ate them as we bounced the ball. Crumbs flew every which way. No one yelled.

I could hear the buzz of the grownups talking. Mumma, as always, was the loudest. They were all "sorry" as they drank coffee and ate cookies and cake. I couldn't hear the baby.

"David, where's your baby brother?"
"In heaven, Cookie. He's an angel now."

Carol Jean

Santa and "The Movies"

"We're going to the movies and Santa's gonna be there," my sister Chi-chi announces one morning.

I don't know what 'the movies" means, but if Santa will be there, it must be good. We put on our coats, scarves, mittens and overshoes. Mumma holds my hand as we walk across the snowy porch and down the icy steps to the car. Daddy has the motor running to warm it up. I climb onto the running board and through the open door. I sit on Mumma's lap as Daddy drives.

"Where is 'the movies'?" I ask Mumma.

"In town. In Osceola."

I try to remember what Osceola looks like. "By the dime store?"

"No, that's New Richmond."

"Oh."

Daddy parks the car in town and we all jump out. We follow Daddy through a big door with glass windows. Inside, I smell popcorn. I see it popping in a big wagon.

"Can I have some?"

11

"Sure," Daddy says, "soon as I get the tickets."

I can't wait. Daddy hands money over the counter and gets paper tickets and a big red and white box of popcorn. I reach for it.

"Tut, tut," he clucks his tongue. "Not 'til we sit down. And you have to share."

We all go through another door and into a big room that's kind of dark and scary. The floor goes downhill. I see rows of chairs on each side. Some have families sitting in them already. I follow Chi-chi and Richie down a row of seats. My eyes look straight at the arm of the chairs, which are stuck together.

Mumma flips down the seat of one chair. I flip it up again. *Whee, this is fun*!

"Sit down, Carol Jean," Mumma says like she means it. I sit.

We pass our coats and scarves to Richie, who piles them in an empty chair. We keep our overshoes on.

"Can we eat popcorn now?" I ask.

"Sure." Daddy passes it around and we fill our mouths with the salty white kernels. It's delicious. I hold tight to the box.

The lights go out!

"It's dark," I sob.

"Shhh, the movie's starting," Chi-chi says.

Light flashes from above the next row of chairs. I'm scared.

"Look up there," Mumma says.

I can't see over the chairs so I stand on the seat to see. The seat flips up. Mumma catches me but the popcorn goes flying. I jump down to pick the kernels off of the floor.

"No, no! It's dirty."

"I want the popcorn," I cry.

"Shhhh." It sounds like everybody in the room says it at once.

Mumma holds me in her lap. "See, that's the movie," she whispers in my ear. I see a big sign with people running around. Daddy laughs, so I do too.

They talk about "Ma and Pa Kettle" but I see people, not kettles, and no Santa's in sight.

"Carol Jean, there's Santa," I hear Daddy say when I wake up on Mumma's lap.

"Where?"

"Up there." Daddy points to the front of the room. Sure enough, I see Santa.

"Let's get in line for the candy," Chi-chi says.

When we get to Santa, he says, "Ho, ho, ho! Merry Christmas," and hands me a paper bag.

"What do you say, Carol Jean?"

"Tank-ou."

We open the bags in the car. They are full of Christmas hard-candy – canes, ribbon candy, peppermints, Santa's filled with licorice or caramel, little green and white Christmas trees. I pick out the longest piece of ribbon candy in my bag and suck on it all the way home. The pretty ribbon leaves my hands and chin red, green, and sticky, but my mouth loves the sugary taste.

I'm happy and I've seen my first movie – sort of.

Oak Lawn School in 1949 -- I'm on the far left, middle, in dark pants with suspenders.

Christmas, 1949

It was almost time for Santa and I was getting worried. There was no snow on the ground (very unusual for December in Northern Wisconsin) and I didn't know how Santa would get to our house with his sleigh. Daddy thought he might have a truck for a backup, but I wasn't sure about that. I had never seen that in any of my picture books.

But then, two days before Christmas, the snow came. It snowed all day and the next morning I was sure there was enough for Santa's sleigh. Santa was going to make it after all. I couldn't wait.

I was wearing my favorite red jeans with the plaid flannel lining and a scratchy red and white wool sweater. My socks were red too, and I was wearing black and white saddle shoes with scuffmarks on the side from wearing my spurs with them when we played "cowboys." I was three years old, but I didn't know the word. I just held up three fingers and said, "I am this many."

In the front room near the Christmas tree, where the scent of pine needles permeated the room, I sat on the cold linoleum floor and picked up my red toy telephone. It was made of tin and the paint was chipped but the dialer still went around and around. I dialed a lot of numbers and pretended to call Santa.

"Santa," I said. "Please bring me my presents early. It'll give you more time for the other boys and girls on Christmas Eve."

"What did Santa say?" asked Daddy, who was sitting in his really big chair in the front room.

"He said he could come early," I answered and started to giggle. I wasn't lying, just kidding.

Just then, Mumma came and got me. She put me down for my nap, on my bed with my girlie blanket. I kept thinking about Santa and the presents until I finally went to sleep.

When I woke up, I rubbed the sand out of my eyes, jumped off the bed, and ran to the front room to see if Santa came yet. I really didn't think he would because my red telephone was just pretend – not like the big brown wooden one on the kitchen wall. If you cranked that one, you got Ethel to answer. Ethel could put you through to anyone. (Mumma mostly called Myrtle across the road though). One time Mumma let me crank it and I asked Ethel to get me Aunt Dorothy, but Ethel told me that my Aunt Dorothy was shopping and wouldn't be back until four o'clock. It was nice of her to tell me that.

But now when I got to the front room, there were lots of brightly wrapped packages under the Christmas tree and a Lionel windup train going around an oval track in front of the tree. Santa really had come early!

I was confused. How did Santa know I wanted him to come early? My toy telephone didn't really work. Or did it? Oh well, I was confused about a lot of things, so I just opened my presents.

The first big box held a dolly, a baby doll with a cloth body and a porcelain head just like the one I got last year. "Oh, boy," I said. "It's Susie Ann's twin. I'll name her Susie Jane."

Santa had also brought several doll dresses for me, and a set of tin "tea cups" so the dolls and I could have parties. If you turned the dolls over and back, they said "Momma." Susie Ann and Susie Jane said 'Momma' for the rest of the day and all the next day.

Mercifully for the family, the day after that was Christmas and I wasn't allowed to bring the dolls to church. There were lots of "point-settas" in front of the church and Mumma said everybody was singing "Carols", but not a word of the songs was about me. I was confused again.

After church, we all got into our 1938 Chevrolet and drove to Grandma Neumann's house. Aunt Rosie and Uncle Alvin and all of their kids lived there with Grandma. Most of my other cousins were there too.

We liked to go there. You could get away with jumping on the upstairs beds at their house. Mumma would never let us do that. And you didn't have to go outside to go to the toilet.

They had a white potty in a room called the bathroom. The potty had a handle on the side. *If you pushed it, the water in the potty swirled around and around.* But "One time is enough," said Mumma.

On that Christmas day in 1949, Grandma and Grandpa had a new wooden box in their front room. It sat on the floor. It was a nice box that looked kind of like furniture, but if you played with the knobs on the front, it sounded like a radio too. Only this one had a surprise.

On the front of the box was a glass window and when you turned the knobs, you could see people in the window. Just like when Mumma and Daddy took us to the *Ma and Pa Kettle* movie, only this was a lot littler.

All of us cousins watched *The Big Circus* on what I later found out was called a television set. We watched the trapeze artists swing from post to post and jugglers and elephants and tigers, all right there in Grandma's front room.

After *The Big Circus*, all of us cousins sang Christmas "Carols". I found out they weren't supposed to be about anybody named Carol. "Carol" was just another name for Christmas songs. After the carols, all of the cousins sat in front of the tree for our annual Christmas picture.

The picture-taking took so long that I got hungry, so I went into Grandma's kitchen. There was a big old table in the middle with a pretty red-printed oilcloth on top. Mumma and all my aunts were gathered around the table, getting the food ready.

Mumma was happy to see me. I could tell because her eyes sparkled. With a little wink, she asked me, "How do you spell Santa?"

"G-E-O-R-G-E," I replied.

Mumma had just taught me spelling and I was very proud. My aunts all laughed. I thought it was because such a little kid could spell. It wasn't until a second grade Christmas spelling lesson that I realized that I was spelling my Daddy's name.

We all ate supper on paper plates wherever we could find room, but Mumma made me stay by the table so "everything wouldn't get messy." I got just a little "hot dish" on my new red dress. Mumma wasn't too mad because it was Christmas and I got a Santa cookie with red frosting anyway.

When supper was done, Daddy warmed up the Chevy and we all headed home. I fell asleep the minute I leaned against Mumma on the front seat of the car and my Christmas was done.

**Daddy, Carol, Richie, Chi-Chi with "the people
who bought eggs"**

Eggs in the Cubbyhole

We had just finished lunch. Mumma had gone to the outhouse to go potty so I was all by myself when the minister from down the road came over. I wasn't sure if I should let him in without Mumma, but he said he wanted to buy eggs, so I did.

"How old are you?" he asked.

I smiled and held up my hand. With my other hand, I carefully held down my pinky and my thumb, leaving some of my fingers sticking up. "This many," I said proudly. "My Mumma will be right back. She's going potty."

I wasn't sure what else to say to the minister. He was something called Lutheran and we were Catholic. I wasn't sure what the difference was except they could eat meat even on Fridays, but you had to be careful about them.

So I climbed up on the stool and showed him how our kitchen pump worked. It was red and if you pumped the handle, the water went in the sink and then into a bucket under the sink. In the summertime, Daddy hooked up the pipe and the water went right outside, but not in the winter 'cause the pipe would freeze.

Mumma came back and sold him the eggs. She kept them in the cubbyhole. The cubbyhole was a really short closet behind the kitchen, under the stairs, behind my blackboard on its easel. I could walk right in there, but everybody else had to duck. Mumma had big crates of eggs and sold them to whoever came to the door. Mostly, they were neighbors and cousins and stuff, but

Chi-Chi, Carol, Betsy and Sarah

Indelible Memories

sometimes, people from "the cities" came and bought eggs too.

One family we especially liked we called "the people who bought eggs." They had two little girls, Betsy and Sarah, who were a little younger than Chi-Chi and me. Their mom let them play with us while Mumma counted the eggs and talked to her. Chi-Chi and I liked to take the girls in the barn, where we would all slide down the haymow into piles of hay, or, sometimes, jump right off the platform above the ladder. They mostly wore dresses and the hay stuck them in the butt.

Betsy and Sarah lived in the city, so they were scared of the cows and even the pigs, but they did like catching frogs. Sometimes they rode bikes with us. Little Sarah rode my old trike. Betsy used Chi-chi's bike and Chi-chi used our brother Richie's. We flew round and round our oval driveway, past the barn, then the house and under the tree near the highway. Just after the tree, there was a hole that Daddy had filled with sand. On dry days, the bike tires would stick in the sand. The jolt would send us flying, sometimes giggling, sometimes crying about skinned knees. Examinations of the scrapes once led Daddy to dosing us with iodine (Mumma wouldn't do it) and more screams.

But then, Daddy got something called asthma. We had to sell the chickens and the cows and the pigs and move to town. There were no more "eggs in the cubbyhole" in town and no more "people who bought eggs."

The whole family circa 1951

Rummy and Popcorn

Mumma popped corn on the stove in a kettle, making a racket as she shook it to keep the kernels from sticking; but the room smelled a bit smoky when a few kernels inevitably got burned. She picked them out as she dumped the corn into the big beige bowl with the brown stripe around the outside edge and stirred in the melted butter. She sat the bowl in the middle of the old wooden kitchen table covered with a yellow print oilcloth, its corners worn from use. It was a Sunday afternoon in 1950.

I grabbed large handfuls of the white kernels and crammed them in my mouth. The salty buttery taste lingered on my tongue, but stung my chapped winter lips. I didn't care. I focused on the task at hand, trying to beat my siblings, Jimmy, Ritchie, and Chi-Chi, at a game of rummy.

I was the youngest, still called "the baby" by my dad although I was four-years-old and a big girl for my age. Still, I appreciated sitting in the wooden high chair with the bird decals on the back, the tray long since discarded. It allowed me to see the cards and reach the discard pile. The table was large enough for all seven of us to sit around it every night for supper.

The others sat on wooden chairs with caning on the seats that was beginning to unravel, intent on the game. We all wore jeans lined in plaid flannel. Mine were red; the others wore blue. Our plaid shirts were also flannel.

Daddy played some days but mostly sat back by the chimney, the warmest spot in the kitchen, smoking a hand-rolled cigarette and saying an occasional word to Mumma. Sometimes he would walk up close behind me so quietly that I wouldn't know he was there until I smelled the combination of tobacco and Old Spice. Because it was Sunday, he had dressed up for church and added the scent to smell good. Back in his overalls by mid-afternoon, ready for evening milking, the distinct aroma lingered.

He would stand there a moment, not saying a word, and then point a shaky finger at one of the cards in my hand. I'd think about the card until I recognized its significance, then lean my head back and look at Daddy upside-down. He would wink and walk back across the room as I won the hand, to the sound of "That's cheating! Daddy helped you."

Daddy always replied, "I didn't say a word," and Chi-Chi said, "Yeah, but . . . " before the "Tut, tut," of Daddy's tongue stopped her.

The boys, who were older, just laughed and we all took more handfuls of popcorn and played more hands until winter's early sunset darkened the room. Then, Mumma turned on the ceiling light, a signal that the game was over and it was time for the chores to begin.

Silverware

When I was about three, I wanted to be able to help with the dishes after supper. Everybody else was doing it and I felt left out.

"What part of the dishes would you like to do?" Mumma asked.

I looked around and saw Chi-chi putting the shiny silverware into a high drawer. She had a handful of them in one hand and she pulled them out one by one with her other hand and put them in the drawer. I was too short to see inside the drawer, but it looked like good fun. So I told Mumma, "silverware."

"When you're bigger, you'll be able to do it, but not now," Mumma said.

I begged to stand on a chair and do it, but she wouldn't give in.

I ate good and stretched for a couple of years before I was big enough to put away the silverware. Finally, when I was five, I could reach the drawer. I took over the job that Mumma hated most of all, but I didn't know that for a long time.

What do you do when the hole gets full?

I grew up in a different place, in a different time, where traditions were different, too. Oh, some were the same, I suppose, like Thanksgiving and Christmas. But life in the

Indelible Memories

1940's in far rural Wisconsin had other problems which demanded other traditions, like with outhouses. What do you do when the hole gets full?

I'll bet you never once thought about this problem that I took for granted. It was part of life. With all seven of us plus occasional hired help and visiting company, it became an almost annual tradition—moving the outhouse.

It was Daddy's job to pick the day in the summer to dig the new hole. It had to be done before there was any chance of the ground freezing. It froze at least four feet deep up there in far Northwestern Wisconsin where we lived.

On the designated day, my sister Chi-chi and I would go into the backyard of our red-brick farmhouse and watch Daddy mark off an area for the new hole. It was always between the bee boxes and the apple trees, although I don't know why. It was important for him to pick a site that hadn't been used before. I think that reasoning is obvious. Recent sites were hard to miss, since the grass was always greener over an outhouse site. As for the older ones, we hoped Daddy remembered.

Daddy and my big brother Jimmy, Uncle Clem, and Ozzie from across the road were usually the moving team. First, they dug the new hole, really deep but slightly narrower than the outhouse. Chi-chi and I stood on the edge and peeked down sometimes. The sides went really far, straight down. The dirt they dug out they piled high on the back side of the hole.

Then, all four of them would pick up the outhouse, which was never fastened to the ground (this invited great Halloween tricks, by the way). They carried the outhouse over the new hole and eased it carefully into position, ready for use.

I was often first to use the new hole, even while they were still moving dirt over the old hole.

I wish it had been one of those "new hole" days when my favorite doll, Betty Ann, decided to "go potty" with me. Our outhouse accommodated two people, sitting side-by-side, a "two-holer" in the local nomenclature. At the time, I still always used the smaller hole, fearing I would "fall in" the big one. That day, I was four and allowed to go potty "all by myself." I carefully propped Betty Ann on the big hole and scooted myself up on the little one. But, as I did so, Betty Ann fell in.

When I got up, I could see her down there, amidst, well . . . all the "stuff" down there.

I cried and screamed for Daddy to help but he was out in one of the fields. Betty Ann had to spend the whole afternoon down there while I took my nap. When I awoke, I found out that Daddy got her out and hosed her down behind the cellar-way. I went outside to see her, but Mumma wouldn't let me touch her ever again, just because she had a cloth body and a hard head that "couldn't be put in the washing machine." From then on, when my other dolls went potty with me, I held on tight.

Birthday Parties

Outside of school, we did little except farm and visit our relatives. For the cousins on my father's side of the family, we all got together to celebrate each birthday. The father of the birthday child would buy a wooden case of soda pop – a mixed case of O-so Grape, Orange Crush, 7-Up, and root beer. He would also buy a case of beer for the uncles. At our house, the beer case was always kept in the cellar-way and the empty bottles were placed in the case during the party without being rinsed. I remember that clearly, because sometimes, one of my cousins and I would sneak into the cellar-way and drink the dregs out of the beer bottles. It made us feel silly and giddy. We never thought the adults noticed.

Mumma always made our clothes. She dressed Chi-Chi and I in matching outfits for the parties, only mine was always red and Chi-Chi's blue. Chi-Chi's clothes always looked the same at the end of the day as at the beginning. Not mine! Mine always got sweaty, wrinkled, and spilled on. Sometimes, they even ripped. I never thought that I did anything different than Chi-Chi, but I was younger, plumper, and not as coordinated – that never stopped me from trying everything though.

Each family brought a dish for the party, always the same. Mumma would bring a hot dish. Aunt Emma brought red Jello with bananas. Aunt Rosie brought a sheet cake, and

Aunt Dorothy brought a plate of sandwiches. They all brought a small gift for the birthday girl or boy, small things like sandbox toys or underpants.

Our sandbox was huge. It was formed by the foundation of an old milk house that had burned down and replaced some years prior. We spent a lot of time in it, building roads and sifting sand, especially during the birthday parties. But I remember on my fourth birthday, when someone gave me a new sandbox toy. It was one of those tin ones that made the windmill go around when you filled the top with sand and it slowly filtered through the toy. But I hadn't even played with it when my younger cousin Phyllis grabbed it and wouldn't give it back. She was still holding it when they lined us up on the grass for this picture. As you can see, I couldn't stop crying. That's Chi-Chi to the left of me with the matching

dress and the big grin, and baby Phyllis in front with my toy.

Indelible Memories

.Behind the sandbox was an old cow-tank. It made the perfect home for the frogs we caught in the fields. We couldn't keep the lid closed tight, or they would all die, so we left it open a crack. All the frogs jumped out by morning, but it was OK, we could catch them another time.

We had a great time with the cousins, playing Frozen-tag and Hide-and-go-seek. When it got dark, we played "Starlight, moonlight, hope to see the ghost tonight," under the yard light and scared all the little kids. In the summer, the yard light always attracted millions of June bugs. They didn't hurt you, just flew into your face and crunched when you stepped on them. Sometimes, we played in the pigpen. Back in the corner of the pen was a stand of young willow trees. We cut off twigs with Ritchie's jackknife and made bows and arrows out of them by tying strings tightly across the twig. We made arrows with rocks for arrowheads and shot them at the squirrels. I don't remember ever hitting them though.

Snow Towns

Mumma was pushing sheets through the rollers on top of the washing machine. I watched from across the kitchen. I had just finished a pretty picture of a tree on my blackboard by the cubbyhole and I wanted to make sure Mumma saw it before I erased it.

The sheets came out of the rollers squished flat. They dropped into the wash basket that Mumma put on top of the big kitchen stool to catch them. They came out white and clean. The kitchen smelled yucky on washdays. Mumma said it was because of the Clorox she used to get everything white.

When all the sheets were in the basket, it was piled high. Mumma put on her coat and overshoes. "I'm going out to hang 'em on the clotheslines now. You can stay in and play."

"I wanna go outside and play," I said.

"No, it's too cold and snowy."

"I don't care," I said. "I wanna play outside," I whined. Then I remembered the magic word. "Please!"

"Oh, ok, I guess. Come get ready."

I wiped the chalk-dust on my jeans and ran across the linoleum floor. My outside stuff was hanging on hooks in the corner of the kitchen, by the door. I sat on the small white wooden stool and pulled on my snowpants over my flannel-lined jeans. Mumma took down my coat and helped me into it. She zipped it for me, but I could twist closed the little metal fastener on the belt all by myself. Mumma tied my scarf and I pushed my feet into my overshoes.

Mumma opened the door and then I held open the storm door for her while she carried the heavy basket outside. There was a fluffy layer of snow all over the porch and the yard. It came halfway up my boots. Mumma went in the backyard to the clotheslines. I went in the front yard to play.

I knew what I wanted to do. I was going to make a town. I got the idea from playing *Duck, Duck, Goose, Goose* in the tramped-down circle in the snowy yard. I headed down the middle of the front lawn, stomping hard with my boots and taking itty-bitty steps. I looked behind me. I had laid out a nice road!

On the way back up the yard, I started the buildings. I put a church on one side of the road, with a store on the other side. I had to step aside for their mailman coming down the road. I looked over and saw Mumma over by the clotheslines hanging sheets.

After the mailman finished, I stomped Mary's house and gabbed a bit with Mary and her mom. I grabbed a mittenful of fluffy snow and offered some to Mary. I put the rest in my mouth. It was cold and refreshing. I was starting to build Tommy's house, stomping fast, when Mumma yelled at me.

"Carol Jean, what are you doing?" She sounded mad.

"Makin' a town," I said.

"Who you talking' to?"

I didn't want to explain my pretend friends so I said very slowly, "Me, myself and I."

"Well, stop stompin' and makin' such a mess! People'll think you're crazy."

Tears welled up in my eyes. "It's not a mess. It's a town," I wailed. "And I'm not crazy."

"Didn't say you were, but you gotta worry about what people think."

That was a new one! Why would it matter what people thought? Thinkin' couldn't hurt anybody.

"We gotta go in now, do more wash."

Later, when Mumma was carrying in the stiff, frozen sheets to hang in the big white room, I pretended to draw pictures on my blackboard, but I was hoping that my real family, the rich movie-stars, would come back to get me soon.

Skiing the Lime Pile

It was a cold winter evening. The sun had set and the moon had risen, but we could see in the dim remaining light from the sun and from the distant yard light and the lights in our house.

I was standing at the edge of the orchard, by the fence, watching Chi-Chi and Richie climb the lime pile. The big pile of ground-up stones that Daddy spread in the fields to help grow stuff was higher than Daddy's head and steep. The yard light reflected the white of the lime pile except for where the long shadows of the trees in the orchard blocked the light. I saw Chi-Chi and Richie going in and out of the shadows as they climbed, carrying long things that looked like sticks across their shoulders.

I was four-years-old and not allowed beyond the fence. "What you doin'?" I called.

"Go back in the house. It's cold out here," Richie yelled back.

"No, Mumma didn't holler for me yet," I said.

I watched them put the "sticks" on the ground and stand on them. It wasn't until I saw them sliding down the steep pile of lime that I realized they were skiing. They both laughed as they fell at the bottom. They picked up the skis and headed back up.

We all had short wooden skis with straps that went around our boots. Santa brought them at Christmas. I wanted to try it.

"Can I ski too?" I asked.

"Not on the lime pile. You're too little," Chi-chi answered.

"I'll go ask Mumma."

"No! Don't tell Mumma," Richie screamed. "We're not supposed to do it on the lime pile."

"Let me try it," I whined.

"No," Chi-Chi said.

"Then I'll tell Mumma," I knew that'd give me a chance.

"Ok, go get your skis." Richie sounded mad but I ran to the garage to get them before he changed his mind.

Back at the fence, I crawled under, pushing the skis ahead of me. I tried to climb the lime pile while carrying the skis, but I kept slipping, so Richie carried my skis in one hand and pulled me up with the other.

"You're gonna go pretty fast," Chi-Chi said as she held me steady while Richie slipped my boots into the straps and tightened them.

"Ready?" he asked when they were tight.

"Yup," I said, anxious to get going.

It was fun for a minute, but soon I was going too fast and my skis went into the weeds at the bottom of the pile and I fell head first. My mouth hurt as I felt something hard scratch the top of my mouth. "Owww," I yelled and I pushed up with my hands and got to my knees. The thing that had been in my

37

mouth scratched on the way out too. It was attached to the ground, a fat stalk of a frozen weed.

Richie and Chi-Chi ran to my side. "Are you ok?" one of them asked. I looked up at them just as the blood started gushing out of my mouth.

"Oh, no! I'll get Mumma," Richie yelled and started running.

"Don't tell Mumma!" I shouted back through the pain.

"I *gotta* tell Mumma," he said as he continued toward the house.

Chi-Chi found a hanky in her pocket and crammed it in my mouth to stop the blood from gushing. Then, she got me up slowly. We started for the house, but were just through the fence when Mumma came running. She picked me up and carried me across the orchard and the yard, and then through the cellarway and into the kitchen. She sat me on the edge of the sink before she pulled out the bloody hanky.

"Oh, my God!" she screamed. "Grab a clean dishrag," she yelled to Chi-Chi. "Go get Daddy," she told Richie. She stuffed the dishrag in my mouth until Daddy came back from the barn.

Daddy listened to the whole story. "Mouths usually heal pretty fast," he said when Mumma was done. "Salt water helps, just like when you have a tooth pulled."

After awhile, he eased the dishrag out of my mouth and looked in with a flashlight. "Bleeding stopped," he said. "It's a pretty big scratch though."

I couldn't eat that night; I only drank water. But I woke up hungry the next morning. I was able to swallow Cream O' Wheat cereal and drink milk. I hated the salt water, but was told I would never eat good again if I didn't, so I gargled as best I could.

My mouth healed over, but left a scar on the roof of my mouth that I can still feel with my tongue. I still ski, but I never tried it on a lime pile again.

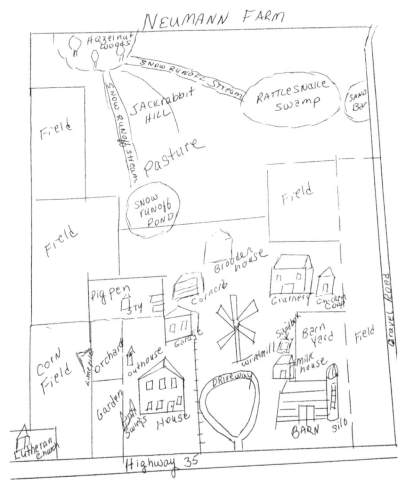

The Neumann Farm circa 1950

On Jackrabbit Hill

Spring in far northern Wisconsin in the 1950's was when the depth of the snowpack started going down, rather than up. It was on just such a day that I followed my big brother Richie across the farthest-away hills on our farm. Only on that day, he wasn't Richie; he was his other persona— "Hawkeye, the Indian Scout."

We tromped off across the cow pasture, and then followed the uphill edge of an ice-covered stream, formed by the melting, and subsequent freezing, of the snow. At the top of the stream was Hazelnut Woods, a small brace of trees in the far northeast corner of our farm. We turned and scanned the landscape from this highpoint of our world.

By this time, late in the morning, the sun was out in full force, warming our faces. We saw another ice-covered stream glistening in the distance. This one flowed down over Jackrabbit Hill toward Rattlesnake Swamp. We lit out, first walking, and then, sliding on our boots down the glistening ice. I giggled with glee as I tried to keep up with Hawkeye.

Hawkeye glanced back on occasion, just long enough to make sure I was following in good subordinate style, and then, he would get a running start and slide fast downhill, yelling, "Geronimo!"

But I was five, going on six, and when I tried to do the same, I fell flat on my fanny and slid on my butt. I yelled, "Geronimo!" anyway, and then got up and tried again.

As the sun warmed the ice, the surface water sent us faster and faster. Each time I fell, my mittens and the butt of my snowpants got damper, but I didn't care, I was having too much fun! We were almost down to Rattlesnake Swamp when I managed the longest slide ever. I let out a roaring, "Geronimo!" when I fell, but then I heard a loud "craaaack" as I hit the ice. I sunk slowly into the freezing water below the ice. I could feel the cold, first on my butt, and then on my legs and back, as my pants absorbed the water. I felt myself hit bottom, with the water up to my shoulders on one end of me, and up to my ankles on the other. I tried to move, but I was stuck.

"Help!" I screamed.

Richie came back to help, no longer the composed Hawkeye, but a scared ten-year-old, yelling, "Hang on, I'm comin'!"

"I'm stuck and I'm freezin'," I yelled back.

When he got close enough to grab my hand, the ice under him broke and he was standing up to his knees in the freezing water. "Owwww!," he screamed.

He pulled me out and we stood shivering on the edge of the stream.

"I'm gonna get pneumonia," I whined.

Richie nodded. He knew I'd had pneumonia three times already and that Mumma wouldn't let me in the water, even in July!

"Mumma's gonna kill me when she finds out," he moaned.

"How's she gonna find out?" I asked.

"We're all wet! She's gonna know. C'mon, let's walk back."

He took my hand and helped me walk back up the hill toward the pasture and our house. The exertion and the noon sunshine kept us from freezing to death.

When the house came into view, Richie muttered, "She's gonna kill me," again.

That's when we saw my sister Chi-Chi and my oldest brother Jim, throwing snowballs on the ice of the snowmelt-formed pond by the pigpen, just behind the garage and in full view of Mumma in the kitchen.

Richie's eyes lit up. "C'mon, let's join the fight, Carol Jean. We'll get real wet and we won't tell Mumma about the ice breaking, ok? Promise?"

"Cross my heart and hope to die," I promised.

After throwing snow, falling on purpose, and putting snow down each other's necks, we ran in and complained to Mumma about, "Jim starting a snowball fight!"

"I know, I saw you," Mumma said.

We thought she bought our story at the time, but the glint in Mumma's eyes as I hung my dripping snowpants over the heater, with the jeans I had worn underneath making puddles on the floor, made me wonder!

My Singing Dentist

After the ride to New Richmond, I was led back into the dentist's examining room by his receptionist, a middle-aged blond woman with a big smile. Mumma followed us in. I smelled the mediciny odors and was looking up at the big chair when Dr. Meyer turned around and noticed us.

"Mrs. Neumann, Carol Jean, good to see you." He squatted down to my five-year-old level, looked right at me with his twinkling blue eyes, and shook my hand. "Time to check your teeth today, Carol Jean?"

"Uh-huh," I said.

"Ok, first you get a ride in my chair." He picked me up and plopped me on the black leather cushioned chair. He pumped the lever with his foot and I went up toward the ceiling. He put a bib on me and adjusted his mirror.

"Open wide," he said when he was done.

I glanced over at Mumma, who was now sitting in the little chair in the corner. "It's ok," she said. "Just do what the dentist says."

I opened real wide and he clinked each tooth with one of his tools as he went around my mouth, checking. I noticed his hands were whiter and smoother than Daddy's.

44

He mumbled a few "Good's," an "Aha," and then a big, "Oh-oh!"

"What's the matter, Doc?" Mumma asked.

"She's got a cavity," he said. "Just a tiny one, but we should fill it."

He took the tools out of my mouth and smiled at me. "What do you think, Carol Jean? Are you ready for your first filling?"

"Now?" I asked. I was scared.

"Sure, it'll only take a few minutes."

"No! Richie said it hurts."

"Your brother had a big hole. Yours is only a tiny one. I won't hurt you."

"Are you gonna give her Novocain?" Mumma asked.

"Nuh, just a tiny hole in a baby tooth. I think the shot would hurt more than the drilling."

"Oh, ok," Mumma said.

When I heard the word "drilling," I was really scared. "Drillin'?" I asked. I remembered Daddy drilling holes in the wall when he was hanging shelves in the garage. "I don't want drillin'."

The dentist must have read my mind. "It's not like the big drills your dad has. Just a little bitty one that goes, 'tap, tap, tap.' I'll show you."

He pulled the shiny silver holder around from behind the mirror and showed me the end. "See this part," he pointed to the tiny end. "That's the drill. See?" I nodded. "I'll turn it on."

I jumped as the loud whirring sound started and then stopped. Nothing like a tap! I turned my head away. "No, I don't think so," I yelled.

"It'll hurt a lot more if it gets infected!"

Indelible Memories

"What's fected?"

"That's when germs get in and make the hole bigger and bigger 'til it hurts."

"Oh, will a filling gonna stop it?" I was beginning to get the idea.

"Yup," he said. "That's what fillings are for, to keep the germs out."

"Oh, ok then."

I was still scared. He put some antiseptic on my tooth and then he turned the drill back on and put it on my tooth. It just started hurting and I wanted to scream, but then, I heard him singing! He sang loud and clear, a tune I'd heard on the radio. By the time he stopped singing, I noticed he had stopped drilling too.

"Good girl!" he said. I didn't know what I'd done good. All I did was listen to the singing. "All done drilling," he said. He put something in my mouth on top of the hole. "That's just cotton," he said. "Leave it in while I go mix the filling."

My tongue went around and felt the yucky cotton, but he was back in a minute and pulled the cotton out and stuffed the filling in, pushing it hard with one of his tools.

"Ok, almost done," he said. "I just needa make it smooth."

I could feel the scraping and my tongue felt little pieces flying around my mouth.

"Ok, all done. I'll just squirt water in your mouth. Swirl it around and spit the chips in this little sink."

Later, I found out that most kids at school hated their dentists. They complained about pain and Novocain and fear. I didn't understand why. I loved my dentist. Sitting in his chair, listening to a concert in his deep baritone voice, became one of my favorite outings in those days before Fluoride in the water. I didn't need Novocain for a filling when I could hear a show tune or two. I saw him until I finished college and moved to New York. Then, I lost track of him.

Years later, I found out that he quit dentistry and became a deacon in our church, where he sang to praise the Lord. I hadn't seen him in years, when he showed up to give the eulogy at my father's wake. When he gave me his sympathies, I couldn't help but inform him that, "Yes, I was still flossing."

Wisecracker

Shortly before my sixth birthday, Daddy went over to the Handrahan's and bought Francie's old bike, if you could call it that. It was a slightly bent and rusted frame with handlebars. The mutilated wheels with shredded tires had no fenders. The chain was hanging off its sprocket and the pedals listed sideways. Daddy announced that he bought it for only two dollars.

"Yuck!" I said when I saw the thing. "What good it that?"

Daddy smiled and winked. "It's gonna be your new bike," he answered.

"How am I gonna ride that?"

"You'll see."

For the next couple of weeks, I watched him pound the frame almost straight with a sledgehammer. He sanded the frame and the handlebars smooth. He bought used wheels and fenders at the junkshop. One fender was a size too large, but he made up for that with brand new tires from the hardware store. I saw him adjusting the chain and the brakes, and then riding it around the driveway to test it out. Finally, it worked. I didn't want to tell him it looked awful.

I didn't see it again until the morning of my birthday. There it was, leaning on its shiny new kickstand on the back porch. It was newly painted, shiny red and beautiful. And it was mine! I only had one problem. I didn't know how to ride.

Daddy said to just go out on the front lawn, put the pedal closest to me up in the air, and step on it. When the bike moved, I was to put my other foot on the far pedal and pump them just like a trike.

Just! That was not the right word for what I had to do. For one thing, I was six and the bike had twenty-four inch wheels. Putting my foot on the top of the pedal was about as hard as trying to maneuver a circus tightrope. Pushing down on it made for an immediate fall with the bike on top of me. At least I was on grass!

I asked Daddy to hold me up and push me until I got the hang of it.

"You won't learn anything that way," he replied.

I tried over and over the rest of the day. I went to sleep crying, "I'll never get it. Never, never, ever!"

Luckily, it was summer, so I had a lot of time to try. After three days, I got my foot on the other pedal. Another two days and I got the pedals moving halfway around. Then, sometime the following week, the miracle happened. The pedals went round and round and I went faster and faster down the lawn and almost crashed into the fence by the highway. I forgot to ask how to stop, so I flopped sideways. As I lay there, I laughed and laughed. I had done the impossible!

Once I learned to stop, I was chased off of the grass, of course. Bike riding was way too hard on Daddy's grass. I pedaled round the driveway and was soon speeding in the pasture with Chi-Chi and Richie.

Chi-Chi's bike was named Champion after Gene Autry's horse. Richie's was named Scout after Tonto's horse on *The Lone Ranger*. "What are you gonna name yours?" Chi-Chi asked.

One of my favorite cowboys was Jingles P. Jones, the hefty deputy of Wild Bill Hickok on TV. He rode a horse named Joker. I didn't want to copy, so I named my bike Wisecracker.

Wisecracker served me well through my entire childhood. I grew into it, but never outgrew it since I ended up only five feet tall. The extra-long fender got a bit crunched up after we moved to town and I went over curbs. The chain was replaced after my jeans got stuck in it and I took a hard fall on the highway. The red paint got scratched-up that time too.

But Wisecracker was still hanging in the garage when I upgraded to a three-speed after college when I worked for IBM in New York. I should have taken Wisecracker along.

Nosebleed!

Just before it happened, my sister Chi-Chi and I were giggling and happy. We were playing catch over a limb of the big old pine tree in the side yard by the garden. It was one of the trees that supported the wooden pole that held up our swings. Chi-Chi let the ball go underhand, hard and high. The sun's rays peeked through the thick boughs just enough to let us see the big white softball as it arched up and over the limb. It fell down, faster and faster, toward my waiting hands.

My fingers spread wide as I squinted through the space between my hands, waiting for just the right moment to close in on the ball and grab it out of the air. But, I guess I waited too long. The ball hit the end of my nose, hard. Blood gushed everywhere. I put my hands on my nose and the warm blood ran down my arms and off my elbows. Chi-Chi came running.

"Are you all right?" she asked.

I didn't answer. I didn't know.

My brother Richie came running, offering the handkerchief from his pocket. It was a big blue one that sopped up a bunch of blood. Chi-Chi ran to get Mumma.

"Oh, my," was all Mumma said. She laid me on my back, right there in the sandy, weedy part of the yard. "Lay still and the bleeding will stop. Just a nosebleed," she said while she felt my nose. The pain caught up to me then and I screamed and screamed before I cried and cried.

51

Indelible Memories

When the bleeding slowed down, Mumma asked what happened.

"It was all my fault," Chi-Chi answered. "I threw the ball."

"At her?" Mumma accused.

"Nuh, 'course not. Over the limb. We were playin' catch."

"She can't catch. She's only five," Richie chimed in.

"Shush now. Not her fault. Not anybody's." Mumma picked me up when the bleeding stopped. She let me lay on the living room couch 'til suppertime, when Daddy came in from the barn. He checked my nose too.

"Bleeding's stopped. Not much we can do," he said. Then we ate supper.

My nose hurt some, but I figured it'd be fine until the next afternoon. I was playing in the backyard, between the outhouse and the smokehouse, trying to turn a cartwheel like Chi-Chi did when the blood started running down into my mouth. It tasted salty.

"Nosebleed!" Richie yelled. "Carol Jean's got a nosebleed!"

Mumma peeked out from the cellar-way. "Nobody ever died of a nosebleed, Richie," she yelled. I felt better just hearing that. "Carol Jean," she continued. "Lay on your back and it'll stop. Just like yesterday."

It happened most days that summer. Soon, nobody even yelled. I just lay on my back 'til it stopped.

Chi-Chi and I slept on opposite ends of the big white room in the summer. In the winter, Mumma hung clothes on clotheslines in there. Our single beds were made up with plain white sheets.

One morning, Chi-Chi woke up and screamed.

I was sound asleep when I heard her. I turned over fast and faced her. She was sitting on her bed. Her face looked scared and her mouth was wide open. "What's the matter?" I yelled.

"Blood!" was all she said and she pointed right at me.

I looked down. My nice white sheets had blood all over them. I looked at my hands. They were bloody too. It was dry blood.

"Oh-oh," I said. "Mumma's gonna be mad."

But she wasn't. She took off the sheets without even yelling. After breakfast, I saw her scrubbing those sheets in the sink with dish soap until they were pure white again, at least until the next time it happened.

Months passed, and then years. The nosebleeds became just another part of my life. I knew I had more than other people, but everybody had one once in a while.

When I started high school, we had a tumbling unit in our physical education class. Our first lesson was to do a "flip" over a rolled mat and stand up in one motion.

"It's the same as a forward roll," insisted Miss Glendenning, our teacher. "Only just let the mat catch your back."

When my turn came, I was thinking about my nose, not the fluid motion she was asking us to do.

I stood in front of the mat in my one-piece blue gym-suit with the bloomers on the bottom and stated firmly, "I can't do it."

"You can do a forward roll," Miss Glendenning said. "So you can do this."

"I'll get a nosebleed," I insisted.

She chuckled. "That's a new one. Never heard that excuse. C'mon, Carol, just try it!"

Against my better judgment, I flipped. I did a good job too. Standing on the other side of the mat, I heard Miss Glendenning say, "See, wasn't that easy?" I turned to look at her just as the blood dripped off the end of my chin and onto the gym floor.

"Oh, my gosh," Miss Glendenning said. "Lay down on one of the mats. I'll get the nurse." She started off, and then turned to one of the other girls. "Mary, can you go in the locker room and get some paper towels?"

The nurse pronounced me to be "just fine" and cautioned me not to do any more flips on the mats. All was well, until our next week's lesson. We started trampoline. We learned simple jumps and we all learned to be "spotters." We lined up around the trampoline, cautioning the jumpers when they got too close to the edge, and ready to catch anyone that bounced off.

I loved bouncing on the trampoline more than any gymnastic move I had ever done, so when we started learning a simple flip, I joined in. The first flip took several bounces, one on our feet, then one on our knees, then one on our back after a simple roll, then back on our feet again. When my turn came, I bounced high a couple of times on my feet and then tried it. It was easy. I got carried away and did it over and over again until I heard the spotters yelling, you guessed it, "Blood!" I looked down and saw the dark red spots all over the green trampoline. "Oh, no!" I said and slowed my bounce.

Miss Glendenning came over and surveyed the damage. "No more trampoline, today," she said. "I'll have the custodian clean it up." She turned to me. "Carol, I'm sorry, but I won't be able to let you jump on the trampoline any more.

"But it was so much fun," I said. But that was the end of my trampoline career.

The next year, when I was fifteen and my oldest sister's kids were little, we were getting ready to take the kids to Wisconsin Dells on an outing and I suddenly got a bad nosebleed. I lay on the floor with some tissues and said I'd be fine, but my sister called the doctor. I thought that was a weird thing to do, but I couldn't stop her. The doctor told her, "Nobody ever died of a nosebleed." I guess Mumma was right.

My nose still bleeds.

The entire Oak Lawn School – 1953-54

Back row: Eugene Parent, Mrs. Jelle, George Rosenow, Allen Englehart, David Krenz, Margaret Kromrey, Kay Palmsteen, Richard Neumann, Theresa Neumann, Dianne Viebrock, Catherine Kromrey, Francis Handrahan

Front row: Anthony Kromrey, Alva Englehart, Danny Parent, Carol Neumann, Mary Jane Rosenow, Naomi Parent, Wayne Parent, David Palmsteen, Dennis Kromrey, Leonard Kromrey, Janice Kromrey

Cow in the Woods

Mrs. Jelle let us loose after lunch. Once she gave the signal, it took us less than two minutes to put the scraps in our dinner pails, and hit the coatroom. Smelly coats, hats with earflaps, hand-knit mittens, long wool scarves, and rubber overshoes were donned in another minute and a half and we were out the door.

"Let's head for the woods," Alva Englehart yelled.

Dianne Viebrock and my sister Theresa were in. So was David Krenz. It seemed the thing to do, so us second graders followed the pack -- David Palmsteen, Dennis Kromrey, Naomi Parent and me. We were the whole second grade at Oak Lawn School.

Once out in the cold, my nostrils were filled with the smell of wet wool from my hot breath striking my scarf. We headed across the dirt part of the playground and toward the four gnarly oaks in the southwest corner. The sun was high and just beginning to melt the snow covering the red clay in the ditch, making it slippery. When we reached the bottom, we crossed the gravel road. The stones chinked as eight pairs of rubber overshoes scampered across. We crawled under the barbed wire fence that kept the cows from roaming the countryside and entered the wooded pasture belonging to a farmer down the road.

Our favorite sled hill was just beyond the fence, but the snow was too melted to try. It was forbidden for the week anyway, since David had almost drowned the previous Friday when his sled runners cut clear through the ice on the pond at the bottom of the hill. Dennis and I had barely saved him.

He had looked so funny wearing Junior Mullen's snow pants that I almost hoped it would happen again. They came up to his bare armpits, but kept him decent while his shirt, pants, and long johns dried on the radiator in the front of the classroom.

Indelible Memories

After we entered the woods, Naomi, David, Dennis, and I brought up the rear because the snow under the trees was as deep as our overshoes. Some slush seeped in and my shoes and socks underneath became soggy and cold.

Deep in the woods, we crossed over a low spot of swampy mud, balancing on a fallen log. David Krenz said it was quicksand for sure. If we fell off the log, we'd sink to our necks and get stuck in the mire and die. But, if we didn't cross, we were crybabies anyhow, so we crossed, scared to death.

Further still, we came up on a heap of tan fur partially covered with snow. It was about two feet high and as long as our dining room table. I couldn't see the head.

David Krenz stepped on it first. It was squooshy. When he hopped down, Theresa and Dianne jumped up and down on top of it, Dianne in her white boots, Theresa in brown.

"What is it?" I asked.

"A dead cow. A Guernsey."

It was frozen enough that it didn't smell bad, thawed enough that it gave when they jumped.

"Try it, Carol Jean."

I was scared. I put one black rubber boot on its flank and tried to step up. The cow gave like a heap of Jell-O.

"Eeow, it's melting fast," Alva said. "Maybe the guts will come out."

I pulled my foot off fast, trembling in fear.

"I see it throwing up," David screamed.

"It can't. It's dead," said the wiser Dianne.

The distant school bell began its slow toll.

"We got to get back," Dennis moaned. "Or we'll be late."

We all ran, stumbling on weeds, balancing on the log, avoiding the quicksand. We crossed the road, slipped up the red clay of the ditch, and sprinted across the playground in time for the last dong.

My leg muscles ached from the sprint. My right hand pushed on the side of my ribs and I held my breath to calm the side-ache. I looked down. My good coat was sopping wet and covered in red clay. Mumma would kill me! I thought of the cow and almost puked.

"Boys and girls, you look out of breath," Mrs. Jelle smiled. "How were the woods?"

My sister elbowed me in my still sore ribs.

"Fine, Mrs. Jelle," we said in unison.

Mrs. Jelle looked straight into my eyes.

"Everything ok, Carol Jean?"

I could feel the elbow in my side, overcoming my fear.

"Yes, Mrs. Jelle," I lied.

Eye Patch

One late winter evening when I was in the third grade, I was sitting on our living room couch, watching TV with Mumma and Daddy. I was holding my hand over my right eye when Mumma glanced over.

"Why are you covering up your eye?" she asked.

"'Cause it feels better," I answered.

"Huh?" she asked. "Something wrong with it?"

"I dunno."

She came over and looked into my eye. "Looks ok. Where does it hurt?"

"Up here," I pointed just above my eye."

"How long has it been hurting?"

"Couple of days." I was getting annoyed about missing the show.

"Since you had that cold?" she persisted.

"Ya, I guess."

"I can fix that," she said and went into the dining room.

I went back to watching my show, but I could hear her rummaging. I glanced over my shoulder and saw her at her sewing machine, pulling stuff out of the little drawer.

She came back once and circled a piece of elastic tight around my head. I squirmed. "Just measurin'," she said and went back to the dining room.

Luckily, my show was done when she returned. She slipped the white elastic over my head and centered the oval white patch on my right eye.

"Better?" she asked.

"Feels good," I said. "But what does it look like?"

I jumped up and ran into my parents' first floor bedroom. I looked in the mirror. "Yipes!" I yelled. "I look like a pirate!"

Daddy was laughing when I returned to the living room. Rich and Chi-Chi came out of the kitchen, where they were doing homework, and giggled.

"Next, you'll be having a peg-leg," Rich said.

"I do," I said and then walked stiff-legged around the room. It was funny that night, but in the morning, Mumma made it clear that she was sending me to school like that.

"I can't!" I stomped my feet and pouted. "They'll tease me to death."

"No they won't," Mumma insisted. "I'll write a note for the teacher to read to the class."

I knew I'd be mortified, but she put the note in my dinner-pail and Daddy drove us the two miles to the school that day. I had no time to lose the patch before I faced the kids on the playground when I got out of the car.

David Krenz called me "Peg-leg Pete."

David Palmsteen thought I was playing Blackbeard and waved a pretend sword at me as he joined in the game.

We all played "pirates" until the big bell in the tower tolled time to go inside and start our lessons. The teacher greeted me with a demand to "take that thing off your face!" But by that time, I was feeling good about all the attention. I pulled Mumma's note out of my dinner-pail. She read it hastily. "Oh!" she said. "I guess you can leave it on."

By the end of the week, the patch was a dusty gray and the elastic had two knots in it from being snapped from behind, mostly by Chi-Chi, but it had done its job. As my cold went away, so did the pain. Mumma made an appointment with the eye doctor in New Richmond anyway.

After Dr. Lindell examined my eyes, he asked, "Don't they check your eyes at school?"

"Yeah," I said.

"How did you pass?"

"Oh, those tests are easy. Just a bunch of fuzzy E's."

His eyebrows moved up his forehead. "Fuzzy E's?" he asked.

"Well, they just called them E's, but they were just lines with some fuzzy stuff on one side. I told them whether the fuzzy stuff was up, down, right or left, and I passed!"

He laughed. "Yup, that's how E's would look with your astigmatism."

We picked out glasses before we went home. Turned out Chi-Chi needed them too, but not as bad as I did.

We went back in two weeks when they were ready. I put them on and Daddy drove us home to the farm. All the way, I stared out the window. It was amazing! I could read all the signs along the highway, even the "Burma-Shave" ads. The cows in the fields were as clear as the ones in our barn. I could even read the population of Somerset.

When we got out of the car at home, I looked up at the trees. "Wow," I said, "I can see the leaves way up there!"

"'Course you can," Mumma said. "What did you see before?"

"Just kinda fuzzy blobs."

When I went back to school in the fall, those glasses made a world of difference, not to my reading and arithmetic, but at recess. When we played "work-up softball," I no longer had to be pitched grounders. I could see right where the ball was and hit it right in the air. I was thankful for my sore eye and the eye patch. They had changed my world forever!

Sky Blue Pink

I heard Daddy's car round the driveway on our farm and stop in front of the well over by the milkhouse. I'd know those squeaky brakes anywhere. I stood on my tippy-toes and peaked out of the screen door from the kitchen. He came toward the house, so I ran out on the porch with my arms wide open. He picked me up and hugged me.

"What took so long?" I asked.

"We painted Uncle Clem's kitchen."

"Oh," I asked. "What color?"

"I don't know. Sky blue pink, I guess."

I thought about what he said. How could it be pink if it was blue? Even I knew that didn't make sense. But Daddy must be right. "That's a nice color," was all I said. But, when we visited Uncle Clem and Aunt Dorothy, their kitchen was blue.

I had almost forgotten about Uncle Clem's sky blue pink kitchen until years later when Dad painted the dining room in our new house in New Richmond when I was ten. You guessed it—he said it was sky blue pink! By that age, I laughed. It seemed like it must be some kind of joke. Mumma laughed too. This time it was pink.

The next winter, we were coming home from my older sister's house in White Bear Lake one evening. As we approached the main highway, Daddy put on his left blinker and muttered, "What the heck?" before stopping for a green left arrow.

"It's green, Dad," my sister Terry yelled. "You can turn."

By that time, the car behind us was honking and Dad was visibly angry. I didn't get it. After fifteen seconds or so, the main light turned green and Daddy inched up and made his turn. After that, Daddy started going home from my sister's through the town of Stillwater, avoiding the main highway altogether, complaining about those "darn arrows somebody thought up." I thought he was having a problem with change.

The year I started high school, Dad came home early one day and told me that the company he worked for had painted all the trucks that day so they couldn't use them.

"What color?" I asked.

"Pink."

That seemed like a dumb color for a work truck, but I didn't say anything. The next day, I noticed one of their trucks driving by. It was light green. It was then that it finally dawned on me. Dad was colorblind, just like my nephew Rick, my sister's son.

Many years later, when my own son, Steve, turned two, I was showing him the pretty fall leaves in our backyard. I thought he understood until he picked up the dullest brown leaf in the whole back yard and said, "Here's a pretty one, Mom." I knew in an instant that he didn't perceive color like I did.

When Steve turned sixteen and started driving, I worried about his color blindness and traffic lights. He convinced me that he could always tell the color of the lit traffic light by its position, adding, "except for those arrows. They're tricky."

Suddenly, it dawned on me why Dad always avoided arrows. Steve has enough color vision to tell bright red from bright green, but it was difficult. By this time, Dad had passed away so I couldn't ask him, but his color vision must have been worse than Steve's. So I researched the topic.

Red-green color-blindness occurs in about 10% of white males (fewer for other races). It is a genetic, sex-linked characteristic that is carried by females but exhibits itself only in the male offspring of the carriers. The gene causes anomalous green and red cones to occur in the eyes to varying degrees. Thus, color-blindness varies in intensity from mild cases of inability to detect pale pink from light green to a condition known as protanopia, the complete inability to accurately identify the hue of any shade of red and/or green.

Threshing

Just after dawn, in the cool of the late August morning, Mumma and I went out into the front yard to set up the tables. Richie and Jim were out there already, placing the heavy boards on the sawhorses. They were making the long tables in the shade of the house. Then, Mumma carried out the fat rolls of butcher paper. When the boards were on, she began to roll out the paper. Myrtle from across the road came out to help her tuck the edge of the paper under the table and tape it to the underside of the boards. They folded under the corners of the paper, finishing the pure white tablecloth. We brought out the kitchen chairs, the dining room chairs, and all of the folding chairs. The tables were long enough for about fifty people. It was threshing day!

A group of farmers in our area owned a single large threshing machine. When the oats were ready, the men traveled from farm to farm, with their wives and children, to thresh each farmer's grain in one long day. The men and the older boys did the threshing. Their wives and older daughters cooked dinner and supper for everyone. The little kids helped as best they could.

When not needed, we kids spent time watching in awe as the men raised the yellow-gold bundles bound with twine off of the open wagon with forks and threw them into the back of the threshing machine. The machine rumbled and oats flowed out of a fat pipe in the front and into a gunnysack. The straw flew into the air from an open funnel and landed on the growing straw pile along with the twine used to bind the bundles together. The chaff was blown everywhere and my nose was soon clogged with it, which gave welcome relief from the pungent smell of the grain, which had been drying for a week or two in the field.

Bored after a while, we kids ran out into the fields and watched the men and boys drive tractors which were pulling wagons through the oat fields, stopping next to each shock. A shock was formed by leaning bundles with the grain-end up against each other in bunches of twelve or so, then fanning out a couple of bundles to form a cap. The farmers threw the bundles into the awaiting wagon with pitchforks and then moved to the next shock. When the wagon was full, it was driven back to the threshing machine.

By mid-morning, the hot sun made the workers sweat through their light blue workshirts, forming dark-blue spots on their backs and chests. The sweat ran down their brows from under their strawhats. They removed the hats and wiped their heads with their red or blue print handkerchiefs. Soon, they gathered around the well for a water-break, passing around the overflowing dipper, gulping the water and pouring some over their heads.

Tins of tobacco were pulled from their deep pockets. White cigarette papers were placed on one hand, and then a pinch of tobacco was spread skillfully along its length. A lick of the edge moistened the paper so it stuck together when it was rolled. They leaned on the well or rested on the grass and savored the smoke before returning to their labors.

Midday, we were back at the house, helping the ladies carry the feast out to the tables. Giant hams, large pot-roasts, bowls of mashed potatoes, and vats of gravy were carried by the women. We kids carried the extras—bread, butter, sliced tomatoes and cucumbers, pitchers of milk, and fresh blueberry and strawberry-rhubarb pies! We all sat together in a long row. Men, women, and children all celebrated the day together.

After dinner, while the men and boys finished up, we kids usually got bored of the whole thing and headed off through the pasture to our favorite swamp, gunnysacks in tow. At the edge of the swamp, we set down our bags and listened for the croaking sounds of our favorite prey. We followed first the sounds and then the plops as the green or brown bullfrogs hopped away from us.

The ones we caught, we stuck in the sacks and tied off the end with twine. We dragged the bouncing bundles across the pasture and back toward the barn, to the old cow-tank behind the milkhouse. We put a bit of water in the tank from the well and dumped all the frogs in. We left the lid a bit ajar, so they could get some air and joined the grown-ups for a bite of supper, some real soda-pop, and games.

Our favorite game started at dusk. We ran around the side of the house singing, "Starlight, moonlight, hope to see the ghost tonight. Wish I may, wish I might, get the wish I wish tonight." One of the older boys would hide until we were all the way behind the house and in total darkness. Then, he would jump out and scare us, chasing us around the house. If we made it to the front porch without being caught, we made a good wish, hoping it would really come true. The first one caught would be the next ghost.

By morning, the threshers were gone, but we ran out to explore the large new straw pile with its fresh lengths of twine

Indelible Memories

hanging in the straw, waiting for us to tie them together and braid them into ropes. Later, we'd remember the frogs and go to feed them, only to find that they had all managed to hop out through the air-hole, waiting to be caught again another day.

Oak Lawn School - the window to the left of the door is in the room where they put the telephone.

Oak Lawn School Gets a Telephone

Everybody on the school board, including my dad, thought we should move into the Twentieth Century and get a telephone for Oak Lawn School. It was 1955 and I was in the fourth grade at this school, which had one room for all eight grades, outhouses in the back, and no way to communicate with the parents except for notes in our dinner pails. On top of their minds were the safety issues, although I don't know what incident had prompted it to come to the board's attention, most likely a sudden illness.

We students thought it a good idea too, at least at first. They installed it in the little room with the hotplate that we used for heating up the water to wash our hands for lunch, which we called dinner back then. They hung the shiny black phone on the wall, just to the right of the door as you entered. It was convenient for the teacher, because it was just behind the table where she taught our classes. She called the classes back to the table, one grade at a time for each subject.

It was halfway through the first morning, during third grade arithmetic, that we first heard it ring. We all turned in our seats and watched the elderly teacher rise out of her chair and hurry around the corner. We all listened in.

"Hello," . . . "Yes, Mrs. Parent," . . . "Picking on Danny?"

What? Danny being picked on? I thought. Danny Parent was the one who always picked on all the rest of us.

"Yes, I'll talk to the children," the teacher went on. "Ok, bye." She came back into the room and rejoined her class. "Now, where were we?" she asked.

The room quieted for a few minutes and I went back to my reading.

"Ring, ring, ring," the phone went again. We all turned and watched again.

"Hello," . . . "Yes, Mrs. Parent," . . . "Not yet, I'm teaching a class," . . . "Yes, I will."

Back at the table, she looked at the wall clock across the room. "Ok, time for the fourth grade. Do the problems on page 88 for tomorrow."

"Ring, ring, ring."

"Hello," . . . "Mrs. Parent, you can't keep interrupting the class like this," . . . "I know it's important, but I have children to teach."

After about five calls, the teacher left the phone ringing and ringing. It was most annoying when I was trying to do my arithmetic problems. After school, another parent complained that they had tried to call, but couldn't get through. Their children's grandmother was taken to the hospital and it was important.

The next day, the teacher assigned one of the older students to answer the phone for her when she was teaching and to explain that she couldn't come to the phone. This helped the teacher, but all the ringing still disturbed the rest of us.

I complained about the telephone at supper that night. Chi-Chi and Rich agreed with me that it was a big problem. My dad thought it was "just because it was new." "Give it time," he said. But Mrs. Parent persisted, calling at least six times a day.

Notes were sent home in our dinner pails. "There are new rules. I can only talk during the dinner hour and after school," the teacher's note said.

But the ringing was still annoying. If this was getting us into the Twentieth Century, I preferred the quiet of the Nineteenth.

My World Crumbles

When I was in the third grade, Daddy caught some disease called "Undulant fever" and everything changed.

He caught it from the cows and he was very sick. At first he drove to the Dr.'s office in New Richmond every day and got a shot. In the summer, when school was out, Mumma and I always went with him. We would park the car on Main Street, across from the office. I'd hold both of their hands while we crossed the street. Sometimes, I'd pick up my feet and let them carry me across, as I had done since I was three. Legs flying, I always laughed for the joy of it. After the shot, I'd beg for an ice cream cone or a Popsicle. Usually, I succeeded.

Later, he learned to give himself the shots, so he didn't have to go every day. I used to watch him. Back then, needles were much larger and thicker than the ones they have today. Every day I watched him sit at the kitchen table and roll up his sleeve. First, he would swab the area with alcohol using a cotton swab. Then, he would fill the big syringe from a glass vial of medicine. Then, he would stick himself with the needle and plunge the syringe until it was empty. I cringed more than he did, and I admired him for being brave enough to do it.

Gradually, he got better, and we thought everything was going to be all right again, and then the breathing problems began. He would come in from the field or from the barn, unable to catch his breath. Sometimes, just sitting next to somebody in church who had the smell of animals on his clothing would make him gasp for air and leave early. I could tell Mumma knew that it was serious, even though she never said it. You could see the worry in her face.

Daddy tried to ignore it, probably thinking that it would get better on its own, but it didn't. Finally, the Dr. said it was asthma, and we would have to move to town. Daddy didn't want that, so he tried a compromise. He got a job at Anderson's, in Bayport, Minnesota, making windows, while Jimmy and Ritchie ran the farm. It was tough work for them. Jimmy was in High School in Osceola, six miles away, and Ritchie was in the eighth grade at Oaklawn School with us. They had to get up very early to do the milking and all the barn chores before the school bus picked up Jimmy to take him to Osceola. The plan got us through another winter.

Then, one Saturday morning, when Daddy, Mumma, and I were all alone having lunch, Daddy suddenly couldn't get his breath. After a while, he fell off his chair and onto the floor. Mumma knelt beside him and grabbed his hand.

"Oh, my God, his fingertips are turning blue."

"What can we do, Mumma?"

"Watch him while I go across the road and get Ozzie."

I watched him turn bluer and bluer as Mumma ran across the road. He was getting cold and I was sure he was dead.

Mumma and Ozzie came back about five minutes later. "His heart's still pumping. Let's get him in the car," screamed Ozzie. "We need to get to the hospital."

"What about Carol Jean?"

"Carol Jean, call up Myrtle, she'll come and stay with you." I understood that they didn't want an eight year old underfoot and did as I was told.

"I will," I promised.

Mumma was a short woman, only five feet tall. Ozzie wasn't big, but was a strong farmer. Daddy was a big man, about 200 pounds. Ozzie grabbed Daddy by the shoulders and Mumma carried his feet and, somehow, God gave them the strength to carry him out the door, across the porch, down the sidewalk, through the gate and into the old 1952 Ford. Mumma didn't drive, so Ozzie drove to the hospital.

I watched them get in him in the car from the kitchen window. When the car left, I pushed the wooden stool under the old wooden wall phone and stood on it to reach the phone. Turning the crank on the side, I could hear the ring. When Ethel, the operator, picked up and said, "Number, please," I said, "Ethel, this is Carol Jean Neumann, could you ring me Myrtle. I need her. They had to take Daddy to the hospital."

"Sure will, Carol Jean." As it was ringing, she asked if I was OK and I told her I was, but I was scared and shaking. Myrtle was able to come over and calm me down. We both sat in the kitchen and listened to the radio. Myrtle cleaned up the lunch dishes. We waited a very long time until the phone rang.

"That's us," I told Myrtle. "Two shorts and a long." The rings on our partly line were different for each party and I had learned to recognize when it was for us.

Myrtle answered, "Hello," then she listened for what seemed like an eternity.

"That's good news," she finally said. "I'll tell Carol Jean...She's all right ... No, the others aren't back yet. OK, see you later."

"That was your Mumma," she said. "Your Daddy's going to be OK, but they will keep him at the hospital for a few days. Mumma and Ozzie will be back for supper. Come on over to our house, and I'll start cooking for all of us."

I began to calm down. I was glad, but still scared.

Daddy came home in a few days, but he kept having the attacks. The Dr. insisted that we move off the farm as soon as possible. He needed to be in a town, away from any open fields and farm animals; the larger the town, the better it would be.

But Daddy hated towns and wanted the smaller the better. "Was New Richmond big enough?"

"I don't think you can get far enough from the fields," was the Dr.'s reply.

"How about Stillwater?" Daddy wanted to be as close to home as possible.

"You might find something there."

So, we began looking for houses in Stillwater, Minnesota, just across the St. Croix River from Wisconsin, about fifteen miles away. We found a house on Myrtle Street. Myrtle Street was one of the main arteries through Stillwater. It went up the steep river bluff and out to the west of town. The house was on the steepest part of the hill. We came so close to buying it, that I was planning how I was going to be sledding down the bluffs. But Daddy had a different idea.

He was still looking in New Richmond, when a house went on the market that was right in the center of town, just one block off of Main Street, near the Soo Line Railroad tracks. New Richmond, at the time, had less than 3,000 people, so none of the houses were too far from the country fields, but Daddy thought this one might do the trick. He called the Dr. and explained exactly where it was and what was around it. The Dr. said it, "Might be OK," so Daddy bought it.

"The house needs some work," he said, "but we will like it better in New Richmond than Stillwater."

So, we began to make plans to move to New Richmond.

Parachute!

I awakened and rolled over, feeling the dirt and the scratchy weeds on my bare arms and legs. My eyes blinked in the strong sunlight. I looked the other way. I saw a thick steel bar, rising up on an angle, silhouetted against the blue sky. I followed the angle with my eyes to the overhead bar. It was then that I became aware that I was under the swings in the schoolyard. My head hurt.

I sat up slowly and looked around. My friend David was standing on the seat of the next swing over, swinging high in the air as he always did. I was afraid he'd go "over the pole" like he did the week before, but instead, he jumped off, yelling, "Parachute!" and then landed in the grass in front of me. *Had I been parachuting too? At least, I knew I wouldn't have done it standing up.* I looked across the lawn and noticed that all of our parents were gathered around a makeshift picnic table, fashioned out of sawhorses and planks. It was then that I remembered we were at the Oak Lawn School picnic.

I saw Mumma in her flowered housedress and thick sandals looking my way and my hands suddenly shook. She smiled. *Good! Maybe she hadn't noticed me parachuting.* It was absolutely verboten in our family. She looked away and I fingered my head. I felt a bump on the back. I looked at my hand. *No blood! That was a good sign.*

79

Indelible Memories

I looked around for Daddy. He was in the grove of trees behind the table, wearing his bib overalls, smoking a cigarette, and talking to Dennis Kromrey's dad. He wasn't looking my way. My eyes panned the rest of the schoolyard. No one was staring or running toward me.

David picked himself off the ground, dusted off his shorts, and walked over. "You ok?" he asked.

"I, I jumped too quick, I guess," was my answer.

"Ya," was all he said before he stood up on the swing again.

I didn't mention the bump and he didn't mention my hitting the bar. *Maybe he didn't see it.*

I must have eventually stood up and rejoined the picnic. I don't recall. It happened at the last picnic that I attended at Oak Lawn School. That was in late May 1956, when I was nine going on ten. It was a week or two before our farm auction and Mumma's discovery of breast cancer, and just a month before we moved to town and I began fearing heights.

I suppressed that memory entirely for over forty-five years. One day, when I was in my middle fifties, the memory suddenly came back. In a flash of recall, like in a waking dream, I knew what had happened to make me suddenly fear heights. I always thought it had something to do with our move to town. Now I know!

Mumma Before the Move

Auction

My sister Lucy was having a baby, my brother Jim was joining the Navy, and we were moving off of the farm. We had almost decided on a house in Stillwater, high on the

81

hill on Myrtle Street when Daddy found the house in New Richmond. It was too bad; Myrtle Street would have been a great sledding hill! But Daddy wanted to stay in Wisconsin, so it was settled.

Now we had to move. I had no idea what was going to happen. In the movies, a moving van pulled up and the men loaded the stuff in the back and drove away. I guess that's what I expected. Nothing could have been further from the truth.

We had to sort everything. Mumma explained how we had to get rid of everything we didn't use all the time because there was no way to put everything in our big house into the little house in New Richmond. Our farmhouse had seven bedrooms, the new house had three, so that made sense.

"What are we gonna do with all the extra stuff?" I asked.

"Auction it off," Daddy answered.

I had been to a couple of auctions with him, sometimes in somebody's barn, sometimes in a storeroom. I remembered the auction man talking real fast, so fast I couldn't catch all the words. Sometimes Daddy raised his finger and nodded and ended up buying some junk to take home. Now it was going to be our junk.

"Where?" I asked.

"Right here," he answered.

"In the barn?"

"All over. We needa sell the cows, the pigs, the tractor, the milking machines, all that junk in the granary—everything!" he sighed at the end of the list. "Even the dog," he added.

My tummy did a flip-flop. "Schnapps?" I cried. "Can't we keep him?"

"Nope, not in town. Can't have him in the house."

I remembered then that Daddy was allergic to the dog too. Darn asthma! "Oh, ya," I said.

We spent weeks sorting everything into boxes, bags, piles on the floor, and even old egg crates. It was a mess! I was warned not to touch anything, because it was all counted out.

Daddy came home one day with a printed flyer. It was as big as a newspaper page. A picture of our farm was on top and columns of stuff for sale and how many of each ran down the page. On the right side was the date and time in large block letters and the name of the auction man, who was really called an auctioneer. The auction was on for the first Saturday of June.

When the day finally arrived, it was bright and sunny. Mumma got us all up early so we could put a lot of the house junk on tables outside. We used real tables for some, and then set up more tables with the sawhorses and boards that we used for lunch during threshing season. What wouldn't fit on the tables, we laid on the grass in front of them. Daddy, Richie, and some of our uncles and cousins did the same in front of the milkhouse, the barn, the chicken coop, the granary, and the garage. I scampered from place to place with Chi-Chi, just looking at all the stuff.

People started driving in before we were even finished. They were looking over the stuff, picking out what they wanted to bid on, trying to imagine how much it would cost. Mostly, they were other farmers in the area, dressed in overalls and work shirts, but some came from the Cities and faraway towns, too dressed up for the barn. Soon our driveway was full of cars and pickup trucks and more were parking along the highway and walking in. I was a little scared of all of them and stuck close to Chi-Chi.

Indelible Memories

Once we were finally ready, the auctioneer arrived. He was a huge man with a bald head and a billowing voice that resonated all over the farm. He wasted no time, starting first with the large animals. Cows and pigs would bring in the most money, and sold quickly.

Next, he moved to the large equipment—the tractor, wagons, manure spreader, cultivator and plow. When they were sold, he moved to the milkhouse stuff—the milking machines, cans, and extra cleaning supplies. These were lapped up by the locals.

The granary stuff was mostly ancient appliances—iceboxes, the remaining bee keepers (some still with honey inside), the smoker from the smokehouse, meat grinders, sauerkraut crocks, and the large pots used for canning. I noticed the city crowd bought most of it. The stuff is probably still moving around as priceless antiques.

Last was the house stuff, largely extra dishes and clothes, but also some beds and dressers we had no room for. As we finished, I came back out on the back porch and met the people who were taking the dog. It was sad for me, but their children were happy. I noticed they had a daughter about my age. They coaxed Schnapps into their car and drove away.

In the driveway, other people were loading their pickups. Some had bought so much that they had to come back for a second load. Big trucks came back for the cows and pigs, some that day, some the next.

And then, all the stuff was gone. Anxious as I was to move to town, I missed all of our stuff, but especially I missed the animals. I moped for a day and then was ready by Monday to move on.

But as soon as I came down for breakfast, I knew something was wrong. Mumma was hurrying to get to the Dr. She had found a lump in her breast while getting ready for the auction and had kept the secret to herself until Monday. Her cancer was back.

Not What I Dreamed of …

All through the move off of the farm in 1956, when I was ten, the whole family was apprehensive, but not me. I was the youngest and I was the one who wanted to move to town the most. I pictured the pretty rows of houses with a few kids in each one that I saw in the books I read. Kids that knocked on your door, ready to play softball, ride bikes, go to the playground, or jump rope. It wouldn't be like the farm country, where houses were miles apart and you only spent time with the kids at school or at church things.

We moved on a weekend in mid-July, the weekend of my birthday, which was inconsequential that year. Daddy, my brother Richie, my sister Chi-Chi, me, and some of the uncles did the moving. Mumma couldn't help. She was staying in the city while she had radiation treatments for her cancer. We all missed her, but there was a lot of work to do.

With the previous people's furniture gone, the moth-holes in the living room rug were obvious. We threw it out and scrubbed the rough painted boards under it. Dark silhouettes where former pictures hung splotched the faded ferns on the wallpaper that covered the living room, dining room, and foyer. We all agreed that the wallpaper had to go, but there was no time on that first weekend.

As we pulled furniture and appliances in through the back door, we kept clunking the hanging wall sink in the kitchen behind the back door. A corner had been sawed off of sink edge to allow the door to open most of the way. The hot water heater on the other side of the door was serviced by uncovered pipes that were hung across the ceiling in plain sight. The dining room floor had a four feet by four feet metal grate over the furnace in the cellar below that would provide the only heat in winter. It lay uncovered and musty in the summer heat.

We unpacked dishes and put them in the upright wooden cupboard. There were no cabinets on the walls. We hung our clothes in the upstairs closets with water stained walls. We hoped the stains weren't recent.

It wasn't perfect, but it did have indestructible asbestos siding that would never need painting and a large patch of Lily of the Valley beside the front porch. Daddy liked both of those. It'd be years before they both caused us problems. Besides that, it was all we could afford in the middle of the small town, away from the allergens that made it impossible for Daddy to breathe.

Come Monday, Daddy went to his new job as a plumbing and heating contractor and the three of us kids were left at home. Right away that morning, I charged out of the back door to find some kids to play with. I saw a group down on 5th Street, just down the alley from us, playing kickball in the vacant lot, so I walked right up to them and said, "Hi, I'm Carol, the new girl over on 4th Street. Can I play with you?"

They looked at me like I was "the blob" from that scary movie that was just out. And then, they turned away and kept playing their game. I felt the tears welling up in my eyes so I kept right on walking down the next alley. I saw another group playing, but they moved on when they saw me coming.

Indelible Memories

I went home and grumbled to Rich and Chi-Chi about what happened. They shrugged their shoulders. Chi-Chi said, "What did you expect? They don't know you."

I rode my bike with the oversized front fender around town by myself, learning where everything was. Every time I went down over a curb, the fender scraped the cement and it got a little bit shorter. People stared, but I ignored them. I figured it would be short enough eventually.

Cousin Barbara, nicknamed Mouse, came over to play with Chi-Chi, so I tried playing with them. But all they wanted to do was read a stack of True Story magazines of Mumma's they found in a secret stash during the move. I tried reading them too. Phew, there was a lot I didn't understand in *them*. Chi-Chi and Mouse wouldn't explain though.

When Mumma came home on the weekend, burned black on her chest from the radiation, I told her about my problems. She said to wait until school started, then I'd find friends, so I waited.

But my bad luck continued. I went through a very early puberty that summer and when I woke up on the first day of fifth grade at St. Mary's, I had a whole crop of pimples on my face. Mumma was home by then and made me go to school anyway.

Some of the girls talked to me. I thought there was hope. That is, until classes started. I'd always been the smartest one in my class, so I figured that would be easy. Wrong!

My teacher reviewed something called the "parts of speech." I'd never heard of them, but I was grasping that a person or thing was a noun and an action word was a verb, so when Sister Patricia asked me what "I" was, I said "a noun", of course. The whole class laughed. I was humiliated.

It got worse. In math, my best subject, I didn't know how to do long division. In geography, I didn't know the capitol of New York. Our one room country school taught capitols in fifth, St. Mary's taught them in fourth. I felt hopeless and I wished I was back on the farm.

The next day, Sister Patricia called me up to her desk just before recess. "Do you even know what long division is?" she asked.

"No, Sister," I had to admit.

She put me into an "extra help" group with Scherry Monahan. I learned math quickly. Scherry didn't, but at least she was friendly. She lived over on 6th Street and even wanted to play with me after school, a breakthrough had been made.

Scherry loved playing Monopoly and eating popcorn at her house, so that's what we did mostly, unless we could talk her sister Kay into twirling the other end of the big jumprope and we could play "school" and "Virginia had a baby."

Months later, when I finally caught up with my class and even made a "touchdown" on the math board, one of the other girls started talking to me. She said I could play with her group, the most popular group in the school, if I stopped talking to Scherry. I thought hard about that for a while. I'll admit it was tempting. But I said, "No, I couldn't betray my best friend."

Daddy, Mumma, Carol and Chi-Chi in mid-50's

I Don't Know, Can You?

I'd always been "Mumma's girl," but Mumma was away most of that summer when I turned ten years old. She was in "The Cities," staying with Aunt Gen and Uncle Willis, having radiation treatments for her cancer. When she was home for the weekend, she showed me how they had burned her chest black. I was left home with Daddy, Chi-Chi, and Ritchie.

The tough part was that you had to ask Daddy about stuff and that was hard. He'd never give you what I'd call a straight answer, if he'd answer at all. For instance, one hot Sunday morning after church, I was up in my room, changing into my shorts, when I thought about asking him if I could go to the Sunday afternoon movie at the local theater in town. By the time I dashed down the bare wooden stairway, taking the steps two at a time, drops of sweat were forming on my brow, not from the exertion, but from fear.

In the living room, I noticed that he had finished reading the Sunday papers, which were piled every which way on the table next to his chair, so I crossed through the dining room and found him sitting by the kitchen table, fiddling with the tubes in an old radio.

"Uh, Daddy?"

He didn't look up, but a "ya," escaped his lips so I knew he heard me. I had to go on.

"Can I go to the movie this afternoon? The one downtown. It's *The Ten Commandments*."

Daddy looked right up at me, cigarette dangling from his lips, and said, "I don't know, can you?"

What kind of answer was that? Wasn't that what I was asking him? But then I thought about it.

Well, I had the time, and the quarter left over from my allowance, and I could walk to the theater, it was only four blocks. So I looked right back up at him and said, "Yes, I can."

He smiled so I guessed I was right and I went to the matinee.

Daddy said the same thing when I asked him about staying overnight with my new friend Scherry, about swimming at Mary Park, about walking down the railway bed to Paperjacks, and even about picking beans for Friday's Cannery as a day laborer; but not about Scherry sleeping over at our house, "No room," or me joining the Girl Scouts, "no money."

I got the idea and as I grew up, I stopped asking him at all. Daddy had empowered me to do anything I could come up with the resources to do, as long as it was safe and legal. So, when it came time to go to college, I empowered myself to fill out all the scholarship application forms and merely asked him to, "sign on the dotted line."

I never thought much more about it until I was in my fifties and my older sister talked about how Dad never let her do anything. Taken aback, I probed into the circumstances. She thought hard about it and replied, "Dad never said we could do anything. He just said, 'I don't know, can you?' You never knew if you could do it or not."

It was then that I realized how differently two children could hear the same message. What had empowered me, had stopped her cold.

A Taste of Politics

As soon as the words came out of Sister Patricia's mouth, it sounded exciting. Our sixth-grade class was creating a newspaper, focusing on careers. We were each to interview someone about his or her career. We each needed to pick a career, right on the spot, so there wouldn't be any duplicates.

I tried to think of a good one, but I was too slow. Hands went up. "Doctor." "Nurse." "Businessman." "Plumber." "Lawyer." "Farmer." "Construction Worker." "Truck driver." All the good ones were taken in two minutes. What was left? My mind raced as I thought of what everyone in town did. I was just about to say, "Grocer," when Eddie did.

Sister Patricia was recording them all on a roster on her desk. The room quieted. She ran her finger down the page, and then looked up, staring right at me.

"Carol," she accused. "You haven't chosen yet."

"No, Sister," I mumbled.

"Speak up. What is your choice?"

I don't know where it came from. It just popped into my head. "Politician," I found myself answering.

"A good choice," Sister said.

I looked around the class. There were smiles of approval. I felt good until later, when I walked home. The wind whipped the remaining autumn leaves across the sidewalk. I pulled my collar higher on my neck and shivered. It was Scherry who brought it up.

93

"What politician are you gonna interview?"

Reality hit me hard. I didn't know of a single one outside of Washington.

"Dunno, I'll think of one." I tried to sound sure of myself.

"How about the President?" she asked.

"C'mon. I can't do that. We live in New Richmond, remember?"

"Oh, yeah."

We were eating supper in the kitchen that evening, sitting around the gray Formica table with the chrome legs. I stared at my plate. The peas were encroaching on the mashed potatoes. I carefully pushed them into their corner of the plate. Then, I looked up at Dad.

"Who would be a politician I could interview?" I ventured.

That got his attention. "Huh?" he asked, furrowing his brow.

I cleared my throat. "I told Sister I would interview one for our class newspaper," I sighed. "Now, I gotta do it." I looked right at him, trying to plead with my eyes.

"How about Bob Knowles, right here in town?"

"Who's he?" I asked.

"State Senator. Partner of Tom Doar, my lawyer."

"That'll work. Thanks, Dad." I began thinking about what I would ask him.

My hands were sweating and trembling as I dialed the number on the upside-down desk phone that hung on our kitchen wall, courtesy of the St. Croix Telephone Company. I explained to the secretary who answered the phone that I wanted to interview Bob Knowles, the politician. She sounded sympathetic and scheduled it for the following afternoon, just a half-hour after school ended.

In the morning, I dressed carefully in my gray corduroy skirt and my red pullover sweater. Red tights completed the ensemble. My questions for the senator rolled through my thoughts all day, making it impossible to concentrate on my classes.

As soon as I was out the door, I walked toward the senator's office through the falling snow. The large flakes quickly covered my jacket and scarf. I made a sudden detour to my empty house to do a final check on my outfit. I was glad I did. The length of the skirt just wouldn't do. I rolled it up at the waist and pulled the sweater over. "Much better," I said to myself and headed off.

I welcomed the warmth of the office when I entered. The secretary behind the counter looked up. "Miss Neumann?" she asked.

I nodded.

She took my coat and then said, "Please take a seat. The senator will be ready in a few minutes."

I sat in a huge leather chair. I had to perch forward so my feet would touch the floor. I looked over the questions on the first page of my spiral notebook.

Indelible Memories

I was aware of the scent of his masculine cologne before I looked up to see him. He was adorned in a black three-piece suit good enough for the President. He ran his hand through his dark wavy hair and then turned and looked right at me.

"Welcome!" he said, extending his hand. He pulled me up from the chair and led me into the most glamorous office I had ever seen. The rich wooden desk, the deep plush burgundy chairs, the walls of bookshelves lined with leather-bound tomes— it was perfect!

He seated me in a chair facing his desk before seating himself behind the desk.

Robert P, Knowles

Leaning back, with his hands behind his head, he smiled and said, "So, you want to interview a politician."

"I do."

"Well, I guess I'm that, among other things."

That took me by surprise. "You do other things?" I blurted out.

He nodded and led the conversation from that point on. I learned lots. I found out that the state senate only met part of the year; that he was a lawyer right here in New Richmond the rest of the time. He explained campaigns and lawmaking, the different roles of the Senate and the House and of the State and Federal governments, how taxes worked, and what laws he had passed that year. Halfway through, his secretary even brought me a Coke.

I thanked him at the end and skipped through the snow, my head spinning with information. I got way more than the two paragraphs I need for the newspaper.

Two weeks later, when the four-page mimeographed newspaper was passed back to my desk, I was elated to find, *A Politician* by Carol Neumann, halfway down column one on page three.

The Oldest House in Somerset

End Over End

What was to be Rita's introduction to the oldest house in Somerset soon turned tragic. My sister Terry had begged Mumma all week to allow Rita to come along with us to the Martell family reunion. I loved the old homestead, originally built as a log cabin in 1854 when Exilda Matilda Cote Martell (her real name) married my great-great-grandfather and began her brood of fifteen children.

The rickety stairs in the cabin that led to the loft attic beckoned me to creep up and read the old *Life* magazines from the 30's and 40's and to imagine a lifetime gone by. Heavy-set and awkward at eleven, I was not yet popular at my new school in New Richmond. I looked forward to old-fashioned fun with my cousins, yucking up about the old-fashioned ads in those

98

same *Life* magazines, playing frozen-tag on the lawn, and taking long walks down along the Apple River. In red shorts and a white blouse, I sat in the backseat of the 1952 Ford Fairlane next to Terry and Rita and watched the red-planked barns with matching silos go by.

Rita and Terry were fourteen and about to start high school. Rita's red hair and big green eyes belied her shy demeanor. She was as petite as Terry who had light brown hair and cornflower blue eyes. Rita wore the pair of turquoise-blue jeans she wore most every day that summer. Terry wore the black Bermuda shorts with a buckle in the back that were popular that year. They were laughing about their friend Navaho's little brother as Daddy rounded a curve to the right and then began to follow the "s" curve to the left.

I looked up as I heard Rita exclaim, "Oh my God."

I could see the underside of a large 50's style sedan silhouetted in the afternoon sun as it cart-wheeled end over end across the road and into the intended path of our vehicle.

I could see daddy give the steering wheel one whole turn with his left hand as he steered to the right. His right hand held his ever-present Winston cigarette. The car swerved and bounced before it came to a dusty stop in the weeds of the steep ditch beside the roadway just as the other car flipped over the spot where our car would have been but for Daddy's quick thinking. It plopped to a rest upside down in the alfalfa in a farmer's field.

Daddy ran to the car and pulled a young man out through the window. He was in his early twenties, and an obvious city kid in preppie slacks and a button-down shirt who probably didn't know the road. His breath and clothing reeked of alcohol as he stumbled toward the road with Daddy. My dad said later that the boy was totally unhurt because his

99

drunkenness had made him forget to brace himself against the wheel of the pre-seatbelt car when he missed the turn and ricocheted off the ditch on the other side of the road.

My dad asked my brother Richie to run across the field to a farmhouse to phone the police. Daddy brushed the clay soil off his Sunday dress pants, which were hitched up with a pair of blue elastic suspenders, and adjusted the brim of his straw hat. He lit another Winston and kept the young man calm as we all stood in the ditch, waiting.

Mumma wore a casual plaid dress and wedged rubber-soled red sandals as she always did in the summer. She mentioned how impressed she was by Rita. She marveled how Rita had begun an act of contrition as soon as she saw the car flipping toward us, so she would go to heaven if she were killed.

Of course, I knew the Catholic act of contrition started with "oh my God," but I didn't think for an instant that was what Rita had in mind. But, when Rita merely said, "Thank you, Mrs. Neumann," I kept my mouth shut.

Eventually, the police showed up and asked endless questions of all of us before hauling the young man off to the local jail in their squad car. A tow truck arrived to lug his car to town just before they left.

Our car was fine, so we headed off to the reunion that was almost over when we arrived. We ate some of the remains of the picnic lunch and talked to the relatives.

But the mood had become somber and I don't remember much. Even the old house and the cousins couldn't quite help us recapture the lightheartedness from earlier. My mind kept replaying the image of the cartwheeling car, an indelible image etched in my brain-cells for eternity.

Mumma (with Dad) had just learned that her cancer returned when grandson Rick turned two on Sept. 14, 1958

Mumma Takes Her Leave

Mumma's cancer stayed in remission for two years, and then returned in the fall of 1958. This time it was uterine, not breast, cancer. They decided against more surgery. I had just turned twelve that summer and didn't understand the situation. I thought that she didn't need surgery and would recover.

Indelible Memories

Mumma went back in the hospital. Dad, my sister Chi-Chi (who by now had changed her nickname to Terry), and I visited her every weekday evening and on Sunday afternoons. Even when the car was in the shop, we walked the mile and a half from our house through the cold Wisconsin winter to be with her. I was too young to be a visitor, but the nurses ignored the rule. Somehow, I still didn't realize she was dying.

My sister Lucy's second baby was born in February of 1959. The nurses let Lucy sneak the baby in to see Mumma on Easter Sunday. It was the only time Mumma ever saw her. I went with them. Mumma was having a good day. She even held and played with the baby and fed her a bottle. She seemed to be recovering. I was happy and hoped she would be out of the hospital soon.

Suddenly, the nurses stopped allowing me to visit Mumma in the hospital. They explained that some patients had a staph infection, and they needed to strictly enforce the age limits. I was upset, having to stay home while Dad and Terry went to the hospital. I continued to hope Mumma would come home soon so I could see her.

One day at school, I was talking to our seventh grade nun, about a field trip we girls were taking to visit a convent. I was saying that my Dad said I could go, "As long as my Mother was alright."

One of my classmates innocently remarked, "You have to be sure if you are going, or not, by today. They don't take maybes."

Another girl scolded her, saying, "Don't you know her mother is dying? That's why she can't be sure."

I didn't!

I went weak in the knees and almost fainted. Apparently, everyone in town knew Mumma was dying except me. I was sad, angry, and felt more than a little bit stupid. Why had I not read all the signs? Somehow, I recovered my composure, and went on with my day. I even went on the field trip to the convent the next week, but I was silent and hurting inside.

On Saturday, May 2nd, Dad got permission from the nurses for me to see Mumma if I snuck in the back door of her wing. It was a sunny day, warm and summery. A nurse was waiting by the back door to take us to Mumma's room. I was totally unprepared for what I saw.

In one month, she had deteriorated beyond measure. Always plump and sturdy, Mumma, who was five feet tall, had at one time weighed more than 150 pounds. Now, writhing on the bed, she was less than eighty pounds. Her eyes were wide open and looked too large for her emaciated head. The white starched cotton sheets were damp and wrinkled where she lay. Some of Mumma's short brown hair was matted; some was standing up on end. She looked like the torture victim that she, in fact, was. The grimace on her gaunt face revealed unbearable pain. She was pleading with her eyes for a swift death. But death was not coming. She closed her eyes, which didn't help at all. She looked at Dad and me with an expression from the other side of the death she must have hoped for. I didn't think she knew me.

Frightened, I realized that Dad had taken me there to say one final goodbye. I tried to talk to her, but she only squirmed in pain, so I said goodbye and left.

The next morning, I was sitting on the back stoop with Terry. It was a hot, sultry, 93 degrees, a record high for the day. Dad came back from the hospital just before noon and said that Mumma had passed away. I had no idea how to react. I couldn't cry. It didn't seem appropriate to say I wished she were alive when she was in such pain, so I didn't say anything. Terry said, "It's a blessing. She is over her pain and in heaven."

Just then, the church bells tolled for the noon Mass, and Terry began crying.

Lucy came from White Bear Lake, and she, Terry, Dad and I went to the funeral home to pick out a casket. We went into a back room full of caskets, stacked high on shelves. I had no idea why I was there. Maybe they didn't want to leave me home alone. The undertaker wanted us to bring over a dress to bury her in. We had no idea what to bring. We felt she would drown in all her old dresses. Dad decided that the three of us girls should go out on Monday morning and buy her a new dress.

We got up early in the morning and went to the fanciest store in town. When we explained to the clerk what we wanted, she asked what size. We all agreed it should be the smallest adult dress size that she had. Mumma had always worn a size 14 half-size, but we came home with a regular size 8.

The undertaker put her in the new dress, curled her hair, and put makeup on her. The body I saw in the coffin on Tuesday didn't look anything like Mumma, but I guessed he had done his best.

The wake was an ordeal. Since Mumma was one of eleven children, and Dad one of seven, just the relatives represented a large group. But Mumma was well known in town, so many of the townspeople stopped by, and most of our old neighbors from the farm came. And they all wanted to talk to me.

I had no idea what to say, so I kept repeating the phrase about it being a blessing that she was over her pain. That seemed to satisfy them. They all said, "Doesn't she look natural? Just like she always was."

That was a lie! She didn't look at all like her normal self. But, I didn't say anything. I remember, I kept thinking that they expected me to be crying; after all, I was the youngest child. I tried to force out some tears, but I was faking it. I didn't feel like crying for a very long time.

The funeral on Wednesday is a big blur to me. I can't say I remember it, and I can't say I don't. Just a blur! After the funeral Mass, we buried her in the cemetery behind the church. It was the same cemetery where we played during recesses at St. Mary's (and where we once buried a bird and sang a full Requiem Mass for the poor thing). These thoughts were going through my head as we buried Mumma. My heart was heavy, but I still couldn't cry. After the burial, I know we ate food in the church basement with the relatives, but I don't remember it.

Dad said I didn't need to go to school for the rest of the week. I didn't care about anything at first, then, I tried to figure out what Mumma would want me to do. I decided that I would do everything that Mumma had wanted.

I started with the house. While my sisters cried, I vacuumed and dusted. While my dad sat and stared into space, I washed off the appliances and did the laundry.

The other thing Mumma wanted was for me to lose weight. So, I started a diet that summer and began to lose weight. I set goals and had official weigh-ins on Friday, just with myself. If I hadn't met my goal on Friday morning, I hula-

Indelible Memories

hooped in the garage until I did. By the end of that summer, I could hula-hoop for eight hours without missing. Even my best friend Scherry was impressed.

But it didn't bring Mumma back.

Fateful August Movie

It was one of those sticky August afternoons, when the heavy air just about crushes your lungs. We had no air conditioning in our house back in 1962, just a fan blowing through the dining room. I was sitting on the floor in front of the fan, reading a library book, when my best friend Sherry phoned.

"It's probably gonna rain soon. Wanna see a scary movie?"

I could feel the thunder about to erupt, making the hairs on my arms stand erect. "Great idea!" I said, "What's playing?"

"*The Pit and the Pendulum.* Based on an Edgar Allen Poe story. Kay saw it. Says it's *real* scary."

Sherry's sister Kay was a year older than us, already seventeen, and I respected her opinion. "I'm up for it. Not sure I want to walk though. Looks like rain any minute."

"My mom says she'll drive us over. Starts at 7."

"OK, pick me up at quarter-of then. Bye."

I spent an hour upstairs, choosing my black Bermuda shorts with the buckle in the back, casual but cool, and a sleeveless white blouse. In the bathroom, I teased and sprayed my hair into a bubble of curls. Perfect!

Mrs. Monahan dropped us off in front of the only theater in town. I plunked down my two quarters and picked up a ticket and ten cents change. At the candy counter, we mulled over the choices before Sherry decided on Milk Duds and I decided on Spearmint Leaves.

Indelible Memories

We walked into the darkened theater, past teenage couples already making out in the back row.

"Let's sit up front with the kiddos," we both said at once.

We found seats in the fourth row of the aging theater. The cloth cushions were torn and lumpy. We leaned back and put our sandaled feet up on the next row of seats – so what if the usher yelled.

We could hear the noisy projectors upstairs as the Mickey Mouse cartoon started. A newsreel followed, and then several previews of coming attractions. Finally, it was time for the film.

The face of Vincent Price on the screen represented horror to us; we were scared already. A young man was searching for the truth about his sister's death. During his search, he found instruments of medieval torture. As scenes of torture unfolded, we screamed, covering our faces with our hands. The kiddos laughed hysterically. In addition to the pit and the pendulum, there was an iron maiden. A young girl was pushed inside and the device closed on her, the iron spikes mutilating her body. The camera lingered on the horror of her eyes, seen through the grill on the front of the device.

I was glad when the movie was over. The rain had stopped and we walked the four blocks home. Making our way down Main Street, we welcomed the sounds of the drunks in the bars, anything to keep our minds off of the movie! As we strolled past the park, the crickets chirped. The smell of newly mown grass was fresh from the rain. By the time we passed the Soo Line railroad tracks a block away from home, we felt better.

Sherry left me at my back door and continued down the alley past Wagner's garage toward her house. I watched for a moment, and then opened our screen door and stepped into the kitchen. I bumped into the floor fan in the middle of the dining room on the way past Dad and my step-mother Marian's bedroom. Dad's snoring stopped for a moment and then started again. Usually his snoring embarrassed me, but this night I was glad that he was sleeping. I did not want to discuss the movie.

As I passed the front door, propped open in the heat, I felt a slight breeze blowing in from the screen porch. Dad's giant fern on its stand in the foyer was silhouetted against the front window. I went up the shiny wooden staircase and into my north-facing bedroom in the front of the house. I piled my clothes on the chair next to my full-length mirror, stopping a moment to look at the photos of Frankie Avalon and Fabian Forté taped on the mirror – my favorites. I put on my yellow baby doll pajamas, with the white lace trim and carried my bag of rollers down the hall to the bathroom. There, I rolled my hair in the spiky devices and secured them with pink plastic picks.

Back in my room, I pulled down the faded rose chenille bedspread and was soon asleep.

As my dream started, I went from room to room in my house, looking for Mumma, my mother who had died three years before. Then, I entered a massive room that I didn't recognize. Torture devices lined the perimeter of the room, including an iron maiden. I looked into the grill on the front of the device, but instead of the pretty young face from the movie, I saw Mumma. She looked exactly as she had on her deathbed— thin, unkempt, and writhing with pain.

I saw the same scared eyes that I had seen in the hospital, too large for her head, and pleading for death to come. Her hair was still sticking up every which way, as it had been that last day in the hospital. The only difference was that now she seemed to know me, and wanted me to help with her predicament. But, I was powerless to do anything.

I awoke, my baby dolls soaked with my sweat. I thought of waking my sister Terry in the next room, but I didn't want to scare her. I waited, listening to the ancient German clock chime in the dining room. Two o'clock, three o'clock, four o'clock passed restlessly. I finally dozed off.

I heard Dad about 6:30, plodding up the wooden stairs to the bathroom. Remembering the dream, I began sobbing uncontrollably. As Dad passed my door, he asked if I was all right.

"I'm ok," I lied.

"Is it your sick time?" Dad blamed all female emotions on that time of the month.

"No. I'll go back to sleep."

When I awoke again late in the morning, I felt heavy and drained. I tried to forget the nightmare but it wouldn't go away. Instead, it became a recurrent dream. I would wake up sweating uncontrollably, seeing Mumma's eyes in pain through that iron grill several mornings a week for the next six years. It haunted my remaining high school years and my college years too.

I never told a soul, never wanting to admit the horror in my mind.

During my senior year of college at the University of Wisconsin, I lived with three other girls in a rundown apartment on Hawthorne Court. One day in the sociology building, I spotted an ad on a bulletin board with the headline "Students needed for dream research." The flyer offered extra-credit points for psychology students. I was taking a psych class so I checked it out. A student was doing a dream study. All I had to do was to think about certain specified objects before I went to sleep. Then, when I woke up during a dream, I was to get up and write about the dream immediately. I was not told the purpose of the study, but I presumed the student wanted to know if focusing on the objects affected the dreams.

I never saw any direct connection between the objects and my dreams, but I was disturbed by some of the awful stuff I dreamed about, even when it wasn't the Mumma dream. Once, I was chased by a tiger. Another time, my genitals were cut up and mutilated.

The project made me wonder if I could think about something that would somehow change the Mumma dream forever. I wanted to have good dreams about Mumma, not nightmares. One night I was thinking hard about the good times with Mumma before I fell asleep.

The dream that night started the same, with me going from room to room, looking for Mumma. But then it changed. Now I was an adult looking in at a scene of our family years earlier on the farm. I was seeing it through one of our dining room windows. It was dark outside but soft light from the overhead fixture lit up the scene of our family, each person doing his or her own thing around the dining room table. Mumma was mending; Daddy was cleaning a hunting rifle; Terry and I were playing Chinese checkers; Jim and Rich were

111

working on their homework. Everyone looked happy and loving.

When I awoke, I somehow knew that I would never have the nightmare about the iron maiden again, and I didn't. The recent findings of Betty W. Phillips, PH.D., Psychology, www.bettyphillipspsychology.com, show that nightmares can be changed by thinking up new endings for them.

As a child and young woman, I never understood the Mumma dreams; instead, I feared them and never discussed them with anyone. From my current perspective, I realize that they involved my inability to let go of Mumma and move on, as the world wanted me to. I believe I subconsciously thought that moving on would somehow destroy the memories, or perhaps deny the pain she suffered – hence *The Pit and the Pendulum* analogy. Of course, it would not, and that is the significance of the last dream.

A Matter of Trust

I was young and scared and sixteen that day in October of 1962 when the fire alarm in our high school started squealing out the air raid pattern. We had just learned a new drill. Instead of under our desks with our arms crossed over our heads, it was out of the classroom and into the hallway. Lined up next to the rows of tall metal lockers, we still crouched down and crossed our arms over our heads.

"Is this a drill?" I asked Eddie, who was crouched next to me.

"God only knows," he replied.

We'd had lots of drills. We were close enough to the Nike Missile Base just south of town that we were considered a class C target, but this was different. President Kennedy had been on live TV the evening before, telling us that the Soviet Union had planted nuclear missiles in Cuba, ready at any time to strike anywhere in the Western Hemisphere. And now this. Had they already struck?

My mind raced through all the facts I knew about nuclear weapons. We had lived through the fifties. We knew all about mushroom clouds. God, I had just dreamed about one erupting in the alley below my bedroom window the week before. It had been beautiful to watch the big white cloud emerge between Wagner's big white detached garage and Hronika's swimming pool ladder shop, but I also knew that if

113

it had been real, we'd all be dead. Not just the Neumanns either – everybody in northwestern Wisconsin, probably.

"Eddie, what good's it going to do to have our hands over our heads if this is a nuclear strike?"

"You think this is the real thing?"

"You heard what the President said."

The squealing of the siren went on and on. My ears were hurting. I thought about Vickie's dad's fallout shelter. Vickie was the richest kid in town and one time when I was over at her house, she took me down into the secret shelter. It was under the ground behind her house, accessed from a secret stairway in her basement. I remembered following her down the concrete steps, watching her open the thick, heavy door. She said it was made of lead, to protect them. It must have been eight inches thick. The inside of the shelter was set up to double as a conference room for her dad's business partners, but the walls were unmistakably metallic. They had enough food to stay down there for weeks, she said, in case there was a nuclear war.

But here we were in the school hallway. I could see the sunshine spilling in through the glass in the doors on the south side of the school onto the polished tile floor. How was that door going to protect us?

The sound of the siren kept going. I almost wished for a sonic boom to break the tension. We heard lots of them in New Richmond. We were just far enough away from Wold Chamberlain Field, which was what we called Minneapolis-St. Paul International Airport at the time, for the jets to get up enough speed to break the sound barrier – lucky us!

But the siren kept going relentlessly. My arms were sore from holding them up over my head. My hands were shaking from the tension. My legs couldn't take being crouched any longer so I sat on the cool tile floor. Then it stopped.

"You may all return to your classrooms now," the voice of the principal droned over the PA system. "This has been a drill. Thank-you for your cooperation."

The tension drained out of my body and was replaced by anger. "God, why didn't they tell us it was a drill?" I said to Eddie as I returned to Mr. Hansen's history class.

"Because we wanted to emphasize the seriousness of the event." It was Mr. Hansen that answered.

"Wanted to give us heart attacks, you mean."

We discussed the severity of the global situation in class following the drill. The world seemed on the brink of annihilation that October.

The crisis continued. The next day President Kennedy ordered a quarantine of Cuba. The soviet ships carrying more nuclear missiles turned around. The enemy had blinked. The crisis, however, went on for another week. An American U-2 spy plane made a wrong turn over Alaska and wandered into Soviet airspace, nearly causing a confrontation between Soviet MiG fighters and American F-102s armed with nuclear missiles. Fortunately, the U-2 managed to get out of Soviet airspace in time to avert the air fight. Then, an American U-2 was shot down over Cuba. U.S. Generals wanted to attack, but the President held them off.

Finally President Kennedy got Premier Khrushchev to remove his country's nuclear weapons from Cuba in return for an end to the quarantine and a promise not to invade Cuba.

The crisis ended, but I'm not sure that those of us who were children at the time, the first sixteen years of baby boomers, were ever the same again. It was under this backdrop that we came of age, just in time for the Vietnam War – a generation, not surprisingly, distrustful of the authorities who didn't seem to understand how to protect them.

A Great Opportunity

In January, 1963, when I was a junior in high school, Mr.Komula, our biology teacher, showed our advanced biology class some flyers about summer science institutes sponsored by the National Science Foundation (NSF) that would be held the following summer for promising high school students recommended by their science teachers. Mr. Komula made it a point to catch me after class and say he thought it would be a great opportunity for me.

With his recommendation, I looked over the flyers and found myself interested in the one at Indiana University in Bloomington. It was a two-part program, a two-week institute followed by an optional six-week research program. But I knew that my family could not afford something like that.

When I discussed it with Mr. Komula, however, he pointed out that it was free to qualified students. Sure enough, the flyer said the costs would be paid for by grants from the NSF and Indiana University. All of a sudden, I realized that this might be the out that I was looking for – the chance to get away from New Richmond and my whole family situation for a while (I was not getting along with my new stepmother), plus learn some advanced science at the same time.

First, I had to convince my dad and stepmother to let me go if I was accepted. This was tough, since no one in our family did things like going to college and they were not prepared for my request. But I persisted and eventually won them over, emphasizing the free tuition and the opportunity to study more science. After they agreed, Mr. Komula and I filled out all the tedious forms and sent them in. My write-up made me sound ecstatic about science. Then, the wait began.

They said I would hear by April 25th. As the date approached, I ran home to check the mailbox every day after school, hoping to see the reply. I was on pins and needles – what if I didn't get accepted? I was hanging my hopes on it by then.

When the letter from Indiana University arrived on April 19th, I was so nervous, I could hardly open the envelope. Did I dare look? When I finally tore it open and took a peak, I saw:

> "Congratulations! You have been selected to be one of the 60 participants in the 1963 High School Science Student Institute to be held here June 16-June 29, 1963. We look forward to meeting you and having you on this campus."

I jumped for joy. The letter went on to say that they were "reasonably sure that all of the candidates wishing to stay for the Research Participation Program from July 1-August 9, 1963 will be placed in one of our laboratories." I was set for the summer!

Dad and Marian were excited for me also, but a little scared too. I sent in my acceptance immediately, before they changed their minds. I knew I had won them over when they presented me with a brand new set of luggage for the trip.

But, they still worried about the logistics. No one even considered driving me all the way to Bloomington, Indiana. It was *way* too far. But there was a strict budget on travel expenses, so I decided to take a Greyhound bus, and planned the details. My sister Terry and her new boyfriend, George, who worked in Minneapolis, agreed to drop me at the station in the Twin Cities so I could take an express bus, changing busses only in Chicago. That sounded easy enough.

That settled, I worked out the details of what to bring. I discussed what to bring with friends Rosie and Mary, and with Pudge, who was also going to a science institute, but at the University of Wisconsin in Madison. For clothing considered to be lacking, I purchased fabric and patterns at the local J. C. Penney store and made the items myself. The only money I had was from baby-sitting on weekends. Every article of my clothing was tried on, washed, pressed, and folded with meticulous care. I was ready and waiting.

The remaining six weeks of the school year passed quickly as I prepared for the summer. Everyone at school, teachers and students alike, wished me luck and seemed genuinely happy for me.

Summer in Indiana

In June, the bus dropped me at the Greyhound terminal in Bloomington, Indiana on a hot, sultry Saturday. The trip from St. Paul, Minnesota had taken all night and most of the next day. I was exhausted, but exhilarated at the same time. I dug the claim check for my suitcase out of my purse and gave it to the agent. After some searching, he came back and said, "Sorry, miss. I don't see this bag, what did it look like?"

"It's light green, about this big," I replied, gesturing to indicate the size. "Brand new," I added disappointedly. "My father and stepmother gave me the luggage as a going-away present." I could just picture the shiny new luggage.

But it was not to be found anywhere. When the agent gave me the bad news, I was almost in tears. He assured me they would track it down and asked for a contact number. I didn't know the number. I told him that I was arriving to attend the High School Science Institute at Indiana University. All I knew was the name of the program I was associated with and the address of the office. I gave him that information. He said they would deliver it to the program office when they found it. I inquired how to get a bus to the university and was soon on my way.

I was on my own for the first time: eager, exhilarated, and totally without luggage except for one small carry-on bag. Indiana University (IU) was exactly what I had anticipated a university should look like. Old stone, ivy covered buildings with beautiful landscaping lining its walkways. My exhilaration heightened.

I found the correct office for checking into the Institute, got my dorm key and a packet of information about the Institute in a large manila envelope. The lady in charge of the Institute office was sympathetic to my plight about the lost luggage. She assured me that they would get it to me in my dorm room as soon as the bus company delivered it.

Tomorrow, she explained, we would meet at 2 p.m., have a class picture taken, followed by an orientation and reception. "Please dress appropriately," she said. Then she remembered my luggage plight and added, "I'm sure you'll have your luggage by noon tomorrow. Most of the students are arriving tomorrow, including your roommate."

I found my dorm room and deposited my carry-on. I took out the one wrinkle-proof brown dress that was my only change of clothing. I thanked God that Marian, my stepmother, had insisted that I pack it in my carry-on "just in case." I sat on the bed and reviewed the packet of information. I was reassured by the detailed schedule with times for everything. Since I didn't see any of the kids from the Institute, I toured the campus on foot and went to sleep early, full of anticipation.

Mimi, my roommate from West Virginia, arrived the next morning. She was a small, exuberant young lady of Italian heritage with dark, curly hair and lots of energy. She was also sixteen. I met her parents, who had driven her to Indiana by car. They were a warm, friendly family. Her Mom, Dad, and older sister, Nancy, all came along to see the place.

Indelible Memories

At her mother's insistence, I joined them all for lunch in the campus cafeteria. I expected to feel awkward joining an unknown family, but the outing proved to be fun. They all welcomed me into their family circle and made me feel like a cousin rather than a stranger. Her father was a chemist with a Ph.D. from Purdue University. Her sister, Nancy, had just completed her junior year at Purdue, which was not far from IU. Purdue was IU's archrival in sports, and usually referred to simply as "that school up north" by the students and faculty of IU. Mimi's family was very interested in where I was from and how I got there. I told them about my family, the train trip and the lost luggage. By the end of the meal, I felt comfortable with them, and much more relaxed about the situation.

My luggage still had not arrived by the time we got back from lunch, so I put on the wrinkle-proof brown dress and the same white "flats" I wore on the bus and set off with Mimi to find the group.

HIGH SCHOOL SCIENCE STUDENT INSTITUTE
INDIANA UNIVERSITY............JUNE 16–29,1963

There were sixty of us, mostly boys of course (this was the 1960s). We all lined up for the picture, and then walked to

122

a lecture hall to hear the drill on how the summer would unfold.

My luggage arrived Monday evening. It had been misdirected to Bloomington, Illinois. I thanked God again for the wrinkle-proof brown dress.

The next two weeks went by in a blur of sultry hot laboratories that seemed to come from the 19th century (and probably did) and equally hot lecture halls that challenged my ability to stay awake after lunch. One day I lost the battle to stay awake and (I'm told) my pen went "plop, plop, plop" down every cement step in the hall. But we learned so much. We made aspirin. We played a game with a computer as large as a lecture room. We learned about many scientific disciplines and we interviewed professors for the "research jobs" that we would have for the final six weeks of the program. But mostly, we learned about each other.

The sixty of us came from across the country, from Connecticut to California. All were smart, scientific, and eager, but teenagers none-the-less. We put together jigsaw puzzles on tables in the recreation room to get acquainted. The girls giggled while the boys ogled and we all loved it. I soon became aware of the limitations of my small town rural background. Most of the students were winners in the National Science Fair. Their science projects had led to connections with hospitals, laboratories, and industry. Their goals ranged from curing cancers, to getting PhD's to do research, to leading Fortune 500 companies. Not at all like kids in New Richmond, Wisconsin, where people "worked" or were housewives.

Only a few of the kids were rural like me. One rural boy spent a whole day riding up and down the dormitory elevator just for the thrill of it. We all enjoyed the campus glassblower, the observatory, the picnics at two Indiana State Parks, and time to swim and just enjoy the campus.

Mimi became a very close friend in those two weeks. Her bubbly, exuberant personality was contagious. She loved to organize groups of friends to do whatever. Jigsaw puzzles, breakfast, a walk around campus, a walk in the rain – it didn't matter, Mimi would organize it. One day, we splashed in the puddles after a rainstorm like a group of four year olds, and loved every minute of it.

But this session didn't last long. Near the end of the two-week program, we were all given lists of potential research opportunities for the rest of the summer; we were asked to determine which ones we were interested in, and to schedule interviews with the professors. This was stressful for me. I had never done research and had no idea what I wanted to do. I just knew I wanted to make the most of this opportunity and stay the rest of the summer, so I scheduled interviews with a few professors with jobs that sounded mildly interesting and hoped for the best. In the end, we were all assigned to research programs with various professors, some at the Bloomington Campus and some at the Indiana University Medical Center in Indianapolis. I was one of the twenty students chosen to do research at the Medical Center, under a Dr. Lingeman, who I vaguely remembered did something concerning chromosomes.

Vans moved us to Indianapolis on Sunday. We were assigned rooms in a student dormitory on the Medical Center Campus. Only three of us were girls. As odd-women-out, I was assigned a room with a student nurse at the Center. My roommate Sandra was a native of Indianapolis. Her best friend lived across the hall. I met her the first evening. She was an attractive black girl named Prudie. I had never met a black person before. I had seen a few in the Twin Cities and on TV. I didn't know what to expect, but I liked Prudie and told Sandra that.

The next morning at eight, I went to the lab where I would be doing chromosome research under Dr. Lingeman. They didn't know much about chromosomes in those days, long before scientists mapped the human genome. The lab was part of a clinic where they were doing clinical genetic diagnoses for the first time. Dr. Lingeman met me an introduced me to his staff: a white Dr., a black female nurse, a white female technician, and a black male technician. This was *not* New Richmond!

After some small talk, I was introduced to their work. The lab was using a special technique to grow blood cells on a culture media in a Petrie dish. During this procedure, as the nuclei in the cells split, the individual chromosomes in the DNA could be seen, separate and distinct. Slides could be prepared such that the chromosomes could be counted. Some could be individually identified through a high-powered microscope. This enabled the trained technicians to analyze the blood of patients of the clinic. They could detect "Mongoloidism" (now called Down's Syndrome) and anomalies of the x and y chromosomes that determine the sexual characteristics of an individual. Normally, people were either *xx* (female) or *xy* (male), but occasionally an *xxy* or *xyy* individual existed with identifiable traits.

I had heard of "Mongoloidism," but had not heard of the *xxy* and *xyy* anomalies. *Xyy* produced a "super-male" with exaggerated male characteristics. "What about *xxy*?" I asked. "They tend to be short, about five feet tall, plump," I started to

125

worry as Jim, the black technician, described a person close to my stature, "with underdeveloped breasts and irregular menstrual cycles," he continued. "Whew, not me, except for that time when I had the mumps, anyway," I began to relax.

I was put to work learning the technique of counting the chromosomes. It was tedious work, but necessary if I was to do research in the lab. After a week or so, I was able to accurately count the chromosomes on the set of existing slides they had given me for practice. I was ready to do a real analysis of my own chromosomes, which I decided was as good a starting point as any. I still had no idea what I was going to do for my research project. I worried a lot about it. Dr. Lingeman had suggested I read articles on chromosome research, which I was doing in the evenings.

Jim took ten cc's of my blood and together we cultured it and put it in the conclave to keep it at the right temperature for four days. On the fourth day, I made slides of my chromosomes. I felt uneasy as I counted them, but came out with a normal forty- six. "Whew," I thought.

But research wasn't all I was learning in that lab. One Friday morning, it was my turn to bring the doughnuts. I underestimated the time and was a few minutes late getting to the lab. As I walked in, I found my four compatriots deep in discussion.

"What's up?" I asked.

"Someone set fire to a cross on a lawn in my neighborhood last night," replied Jim.

"Why would they do that?" I asked naively.

I had never heard of a cross burning. We discussed the racial tensions in Indianapolis that summer. I had no idea things were that bad.

That evening, I mentioned to my roommate Sandra how upset I was over the cross burning incident, and how fearful my black colleagues were. I explained how I could not understand what was behind the tensions.

Sandra had grown up in a "changing" neighborhood and explained how fearful the whites in these neighborhoods were for their economic well-being. She explained how, once a black family moved in to a white neighborhood, some of the people would move out. This began to drop the housing values, so even the people who liked the black families began selling their homes before the values dropped further, thus, beginning a cycle of poverty and fear. It was more about economics than inherent racial hatred. As I began to understand the background underlying the tensions, my feelings became clearer and I was more sympathetic to both sides of the argument.

One other student from the Institute was also doing research under Dr. Lingeman, albeit not in the same lab. Chip Land was also sixteen, but looked fourteen at best. He was a thin young man from Cincinnati, with blond hair that had a thatch sticking up in the back that gave him a Dennis the Menace kind of look. As I got to know Chip, I understood how much that look suited him. Chip always wore "nerdy" kind of clothes. A white button-down shirt with a pocket protector and the kind of nondescript dress-pants that engineers always wear, with a slide-rule tucked in the back pocket.

Chip was doing cancer research using white mice as subjects. Chip loved working in the lab as a way to learn new things and as a way to impress people with his intelligence. It was Chip that bailed me out on the research project. A kindred spirit, he suggested I work with him, thinking that if we were

127

able to grow the chromosomes of the affected mice, we might be able to track the genetic effects of the cancers. I was grateful, and very relieved. Although somewhat of a loner, Chip welcomed the companionship, and the chance to bounce ideas off me.

Chip got a donation of research mice from Lily Laboratories in Indianapolis after he presented his research ideas. They also gave him a single mouse that was the lone survivor of a strain of mice that they had been using for their own experiments with cancer. It was not known why this mouse had survived when all its siblings got tumors and died.

Chip and I loved that mouse, named it Bertha, and kept it as a pet. One day, when we were making slides, a drop of the purple stain we were using fell on Bertha. That gave us a great idea. We dyed Bertha a lovely lavender color. She was so cute, we took her around the building to show her off. We did not expect the screams we got from the hematology lab nurses. "Get that rodent out of here or we will kill it," they screamed. We kept Bertha hidden for some time. We expected her to die of cancer that summer, but she never did.

Chip and I got to know Dr. Lingeman and his wife quite well that summer. His wife was also a research doctor at the IU Medical Center, and ran a laboratory in the next building. They invited us over for dinner, where we discussed our research and our futures. They both encouraged us to continue our research.

A group of us from the Institute became fast friends. Camille and Rhea, the other two girls at the Medical Center, were both from Indiana and spent most weekends at home. Tom, Chip, Bill and I were from out of state and spent our weekends in the dorm. We swam in the indoor campus pool, and then we went up on the dorm roof to get tanned. As a diversion, we played cards and I was soon in great demand as a Euchre partner. (My father had taught me well.)

The campus buildings were connected by underground tunnels, which were convenient but scary at night, especially after Chip and Tom spooked us out. But it was much more frightening off campus as the race riots continued throughout the summer.

We stayed on campus mostly, but took a few outings off campus. As a group, we saw the movies *Cleopatra* and *How the West Was Won*. My roommate and some friends took me with them to Raceway Park to see an auto race. No one had money for admission, but one of Sandra's friends knew a great place to see the race over the fence. We walked through poison ivy to get to a tree near the fence. As we sat on the branches, we got a great view of the race. We couldn't hear the announcements, so we needed to track the cars ourselves. I was the only one who knew which car won at the end. Sandra's friends didn't believe it, but I was right.

Throughout the summer, I received an almost daily letter from my stepmother, Marian. A big part of the reason I had for attending the Science Institute in the first place was to get away from the situation. Now, this person was writing me nearly every day. They were cheerful, newsy letters about what was going on in New Richmond, about family picnics and birthdays, about my nephew, Ricky, getting his first pair of glasses, about cousin Rose Mary's wedding, and about what Marian thought about things. Marian had only a sixth grade education but wrote wonderful letters. She poured her heart out in a stream of consciousness that told about everything she thought and what she thought about everybody. I began writing back in kind, as often as I could and the dialogue that ensued gave us a chance to know each other so well that, by the end of the summer, most of the tension was gone.

We in Indianapolis maintained contact with the rest of the group in Bloomington via writing letters (it was long before cheap long-distance and cell phones) and occasional outings with them. We went to the Brown County Playhouse in southern Indiana to see *The Pursuit of Happiness*. We went to Yellowstone State Park for a picnic followed by hiking, and canoeing.

As we were exploring the park, we found the entrance to a cave. Some of the local boys had been to the park before and encouraged us to do some amateur spelunking. Tom, Chip, Mimi, and I were intrigued. The cave entrance was wide, so we went in.

We set foot into a large chamber. Once our eyes adjusted to the dim light, we could see stalactites and stalagmites forming in the dampness. The uneven surfaces of both the floor and the walls made movement precarious. We felt our way slowly, arms extended and feet shuffling. Tom took advantage of the darkness to scare us into believing there might be a bear in one of the recesses.

After a short distance, the cave branched out into multiple low tunnels, and became wet and dark. We hunched over and had trudged a short distance down one tunnel when we scared a dozen or so bats that had been sleeping on the ceiling. As they flew at us, I stood up and bonked my head on the cave ceiling. At that point, I decided spelunking without a lantern was not a good idea and headed out. The rest of the gang followed.

As we returned to the group at the picnic site, we reported the cave incident as the coolest thing, and became known as the brave souls that had survived the caves and the bats. The Yellowstone picnic was the best because we knew each other well by then, and trusted each other. We were able to kid around, even about bats, and enjoy the late summer evening campfire to the fullest, making up songs about our adventures in the caves, and in the laboratories of IU.

At the end of the Institute, we wrote final reports on our research and presented them to the full group on the Bloomington Campus. My mouse chromosome research had not been successful and I feared not having anything to report. But, as I wrote, I realized how much I had learned about both chromosomes and mice. Dr. Lingeman pointed out the value of reporting even unsuccessful research, to aid in future trials. In the end, my paper sounded quite scholarly. As I prepared to present the results, I borrowed pictures of chromosomes from *Scientific American* magazine, and even packed up Bertha for the presentation as a prop.

When we arrived in Bloomington, we were nervous, but confident. As a group, we had learned much about research. We had also learned much about ourselves, and the world. We presented breakthroughs, setbacks, and tentative learnings. My chromosome talk went well. Bertha was the star of the show. Chip followed with his cancer research talk. He had not found a cure for cancer that summer, but he was planning to continue his work the following summer.

What I learned personally that summer went way beyond research. I learned that the whole world was open to

me. From that summer on, the whole world was my stage and
the opportunities were endless.

Dad's Writing Desk

I first remember the desk in the corner of the front room, back on the farm when I was about four or five. One side of the desk had a bookcase covered in glass that had important-looking books in it. My favorite was *Fifty Famous Fairy Tales*.

It had a brown cover with orange writing on it. I tried hard to talk my brothers and sisters into reading the stories to me. My favorite was the one about the shoemaker's children.

My next favorite was *Hansel and Gretel*. I loved the part where they left a trail of crumbs in the woods. But the best part wasn't the story itself, but the warm feeling I had, just being with my siblings on the couch.

Ritchie and Chi-Chi (who later changed her nickname to Terry) read often. It was harder to pin Jimmy down, except for the time he broke his leg in eighth grade. Then, he read every day, sometimes making up stories about Paul Bunyon instead of reading, but it didn't matter to me. Lucy was in high school, so she didn't read much. She had boyfriends to see. I longed to be old enough for boyfriends too.

The other half of the desk had a slanted top with a flip-down writing table that covered several cubbyhole bins, and three drawers below. My dad kept important papers in there, like income tax forms, checks, and bank statements. It's also where he kept his pipe tobacco and pipe cleaners. It always smelled of Prince Albert.

When we moved to the town of New Richmond when I was ten, it moved with us and was placed in the foyer, between the front door and the staircase to the second floor. My dad's favorite potted fern on a wooden stand sat in the dimly-lit north window next to it. Jimmy was in the U.S. Navy when we moved. He sent us all a full set of the Encyclopedia Americana. My dad squeezed a bookshelf in between the fern and the desk for it.

In New Richmond, the desk took on some new meanings. My mother was dying of breast cancer. The insurance didn't pay for all the radiation treatments and hospitalizations so we were poor. My dad was a product of the Great Depression and he didn't believe in borrowing money for anything, not even the house in New Richmond. We had to find one that cost less than the equity in the farm. Thus, it pained him to sit as his desk and fill out the loan forms, but we had to eat.

When he came back from the bank, he showed me the crisp one hundred dollar bills they gave him before he hid them in the desk. I had never seen one before.

When I needed pipe cleaners for a craft project at St. Mary's school, my mother didn't give me the money to buy them. She sent me into my father's desk.

"But they're all white. I need red and green too," I said.

"You can dye them with tempura paint," she said.

It worked, sort of. They didn't look like the ones my friends bought, but they worked, and were free!

When we met the Heibels down the street, we had no idea how closely our worlds would intertwine. They were in their early eighties when we moved to New Richmond. Ritchie met old Mr. Heibel one day, who insisted on being called Grandpa. Ritchie noticed the wooden lawn ornaments in his yard. Grandpa showed Ritchie how to make them in his garage, tracing patterns on plywood and cutting them with a coping saw. Ritchie's favorites were the animals. Soon he was making and painting squirrels, deer, and ducks, and our lawn was soon covered with them.

Ritchie had problems living in town and attending the larger high school. When his hands began shaking uncontrollably, my dad was at his wit's end. The doctor found nothing wrong. Mr. Heibel had a son Frank, who lived out on a farm near the town of Clear Lake, Wisconsin, about fifteen miles from New Richmond. Frank and his wife, Dorothy, had always wanted children, but were unable to have children of their own. Once, when Dad was talking to Grandpa Heibel,

Indelible Memories

Grandpa brought up the subject of Ritchie's shaking. Dad thought it was because we had left the farm and the school in town was too stressful. Grandpa mentioned that his son Frank could always use help on the farm. Dad had met Frank and knew him to be a decent man, so he pursued it.

Ritchie spent the next three years living on the farm with Frank and Dorothy Heibel. There he helped with the farm chores and went to school at Clear Lake High School, a much smaller school than New Richmond High School. It did not get rid of his shakes, which he has to this day, but he was much happier living out in the country. We visited him on the farm quite often and the families became close friends.

When Frank took one of his cross-country summer drives, he purchased a wooden cutout of our family name, Neumann. It was in cursive script, cut from one piece of light oak with a jigsaw. They are common now, but that was the first time we had seen one. My dad gave it the place of honor on top of the desk in the foyer.

I remember the desk again when I was finishing high school and looking for a scholarship for college. I was thinking about commuting to our local state college, about fifteen miles away. My guidance counselor, Mr. Erickson, thought that I should aim my sights higher. He suggested that I apply to the University of Wisconsin in Madison.

"But we don't have any money," I said. "I'm not even sure I can scrape together enough for River Falls."

"But you're going to be the valedictorian of the class. You'll be able to get scholarship money," he insisted. "I'll give you the forms to fill out, and an application for the UW – Madison."

"I'll need one for River Falls too," I replied, adding, "Just in case."

"No, you won't need it," he was assured of that.

But I wasn't so sure. "Suppose I don't get the scholarship money and I need to go to River Falls. When would I need to apply?"

"About September 20th."

"But they start September 15th."

"That's my point exactly," he said. "They'd take you even if you applied late."

So, I took the applications home. That evening, I looked them over. The one for the UW – Madison looked pretty straight forward, but the scholarship application looked impossible. How was I ever going to get all that data out of my dad? I knew he wouldn't fill it out. I thought it was hopeless.

Then one Saturday morning I had an idea. I looked through the drawers in my dad's desk and found the tax forms for the necessary years to complete the scholarship application. I looked through the rest of his desk and found more: bank statements, property tax receipts – an entire financial history of the family.

Armed with all this, I spent the rest of the weekend huddled up in my room with the application and the financial forms. By Monday morning, I had the whole form filled out. I approached my dad with the form and asked him to "please sign here."

"What's this?" he asked.

"Scholarship application."

"Where'd you get all this data?" he asked, flipping through the form.

"Tax papers in the desk," I replied, offering as little information as possible.

Indelible Memories

My strategy worked. He signed the form and I was able to submit it by the deadline. That desk set up my career.

When my dad died, my sister thought that I should inherit that desk. It still sat in the foyer with the Neumann cutout on top. The fern was still alive, even though more than forty years had passed since we left the farm. The books were still inside, including *Fifty Famous Fairy Tales*.

My husband and I rented a trailer. My sister's husband helped us pack the desk, books and all, into the trailer and we drove it down to our summer home, a condominium in Williams Bay, Wisconsin, on Lake Geneva where we now live in retirement. There, it has a place of honor in the living room, on the wall cattycorner from the fireplace. The books are still inside, and the Neumann cutout is still on top.

Out of the Attic

I stretched one sneakered foot onto the edge of the access hole to the attic and pushed hard with both hands, attempting to thrust my body into the attic. But my right hand lost its grip and slipped slowly off of the wooden beam. All I could do was watch it slide.

I was certain I would be killed as I fell toward the stepladder several feet below. Instead, I was intercepted by the ladder's paint tray. As my butt hit the wooden tray, it went craa...aack, but didn't break through. I found myself sitting on the tray, facing away from the ladder, totally unscathed with the exception of my feminine ego.

First, I laughed. Then, I tried to turn to grab the ladder to ease myself down, but the tray cracked again. I was afraid it would break off and dump me the five and a half feet to the floor by the doorway, scratching me up in the process or sending my head into the doorframe. I was stranded.

"Dad, Dad, help!" I yelled.

I heard Dad saunter up the stairs. It was as fast as his fifty years and beer belly would allow, I guessed. He saw my precarious position and frowned.

"You needa be more careful getting down from the attic," he said, a lot of words for him. Maybe he was mad.

"But, Dad, I was going up."

"Oh."

Not "oh-oh," or "oops," just "oh."

He reached up and helped me down, then sauntered back where he came from, leaving me with the open attic hole, the ladder with the splintered paint tray, and not a clue as to what to do next.

What did that man expect of me? Super-woman?

My hands were shaking and my knees were buckling when I looked back up at the hole in the eight and a half foot ceiling of our ancient house. I was five feet tall and eighteen years old, and wanting to search the attic for something in which to pack my stuff to take to college. I knew there was an old green trunk up there and I thought about another try but I was too scared. Well, mostly I was too mad – too mad at Dad to ask for help and too mad at myself for failing.

Determined to find that trunk and get off to college, I climbed up the ladder again, but barely managed to slide the hatch back over the hole before retreating. I folded the ladder and shoved it back into the hall closet, ignoring the splintered tray, and went in my bedroom and cried.

My sister Terry came home later and we had supper; me glancing at Dad from time to time, and him frowning back at me, neither saying a word. I never mentioned the incident again and neither did Dad.

Terry and her husband, George, retrieved the trunk for me on Sunday while Dad was out fishing. The trunk is still in my garage forty-two years later. I never tried to ascend an attic again.

Danny Boy

Laura Lee was a phenom! The striking blond with the space between her front teeth waltzed into my life during my freshman year of college and skipped out just as fast. But she left a lasting imprint on my soul.

I first met Laura when she was playing the piano in the first floor lounge of our dorm. The piece was delightful. I figured it was classical, but I had never heard classical music played so animatedly. I asked her after what composer it was and she answered, "Rachmaninoff, the Russian composer."

I mentioned that, "I always wished I'd had piano lessons, but we couldn't afford them." I'd said that many times to many people and nothing ever came of it. I felt I was about as musical as a table. But Laura was a music major who had also lost her mother when she was a child. She was raised by her elderly grandmother in northern Wisconsin, so we did have some things in common.

She refused to accept my lack of lessons and began teaching me the piano. She found a piano primmer in her musical bag of tricks and soon had me plunking out the notes to a song about swans on a lake with both hands. I loved it!

She continued my lessons even after she broke her right wrist. She only needed one hand to teach. In fact, she could play classical pieces with one hand, improvising the notes so one hand sounded like two.

It was when she heard my attempt to sing the words that she declared me tone deaf. Singing was not something we had in common. But then she happened to be walking past my dorm room one day and heard me singing *Danny Boy*.

I was sitting on my bed, reminiscing about my days at St. Mary's School with my roommate, when I remembered that song that we had rehearsed so many times in the spring of 1959 for the biggest concert ever held among the Catholic schools in the area.

When I began belting out the song, "Oh Danny Boy, the pipes, the pipes are calling," Laura Lee poked her head in my room. "Carol?" she asked. She looked dumbfounded. "You're . . . you're singing that perfectly. How can that be?"

I told her about the seventh grade concert that I had rehearsed for so long, but had never actually performed because my mother died the Sunday before the concert.

Laura declared that I was not tone deaf after all, just not trained. She began my training then and there. I'm sure I would have learned if she had stayed at the University of Wisconsin, but she started my lessons just before semester break.

I went home to New Richmond for the break. When I returned, I couldn't find Laura or our friend Peggy. Peggy's mother called me to ask if I knew where they went. She hadn't heard from Peggy since the start of the break. I had no idea. Laura's grandmother called too, but I hadn't a clue where they had gone.

After several days, Peggy called me and said they had run away to New York City together, where Laura wanted to attend the Julliard School of Music because she had flunked Sociology 101 and didn't feel that she fit in at the university. Peggy said that Laura was over at the school, demonstrating her piano to someone named Leonard Bernstein. Peggy didn't know who he was. When I explained to her how famous he was, she was flabbergasted.

Peggy came back to school, but Laura stayed in New York and attended Julliard. I never did get those voice lessons, so I can still only sing *Danny Boy*.

Laura did reenter our lives briefly three years later when we were seniors. She invited us to her wedding. When she finished Julliard, she moved back to Wisconsin and married the sociology professor who taught the course she flunked freshman year. I last saw her pushing her son past our apartment in a stroller. She was truly a phenom!

The Morning That Changed My World

My whole world changed in one morning. It was a cold, dark, November day in 1966. I walked into the lower level of the Sociology Building at the University of Wisconsin to get a cup of coffee from the vending machine down there before my first class. It was the best coffee machine on campus in my opinion, and I had tried most.

It was early and I was sleepy. A loud male voice started me awake.

"Where do you think you're going?" he snapped.

I looked up and faced a police line. I was scared.

"Uh, to get a cup of coffee," I mumbled..

"Better get it somewhere else," he said. He was angry. I had no idea what was going on. I looked up and saw some signs saying, "DOW Chemical Interviews." I had heard they would be doing on-campus interviews, but I had thought nothing of it. I turned to walk out and spotted a classmate. He explained that they were expecting protests of DOW, due to the use of napalm in Nam. This incendiary defoliant was being used to catch the Vietnamese in the jungles before they could strike. It was also causing lots of injuries to women and children. It was a product of DOW. There had been lots of

144

protests at the University of California Berkeley campus already.

At this time, I was still wearing penny loafers and worrying about having knee socks that matched my sweater. Worrying about defoliants in the jungles of Vietnam was the farthest thing from my thoughts.

The protests started and campus life was never the same again. During the first protest, I was talked into joining the anti-demonstration demonstration and proudly carried a sign that read, "DOW Chemical also makes soap." The only protest march I had ever seen first hand was the minor protest against Barry Goldwater when he talked on the steps of the Wisconsin capitol building in the fall of 1964. He was running against President Johnson as a "hawk" in favor of using tactical nuclear weapons in the Vietnam War. I had gone to watch only.

But other students began serious protest and the police struck back. One day, as I walked from Bascom Hall down the hill to my math class at Van Vleck, one of my friends walked toward me, crying. I wanted to stop her and ask what was wrong, but then, I started to cry too. I looked around. Every single student was crying. It was tear gas! Some students were protesting on University Avenue and the cops had tear-gassed the whole area. That's when I agreed with those who called the police "pigs."

As the school year wore on, I became more and more anti-war, and more and more in favor of the protests as the only way to get attention paid to the causes of students. We all were!

We protested companies and politicians who supported the Vietnam War, which seemed to be killing a generation of young men for no good reason. The United

Indelible Memories

States seemed to no longer be into winning the war, but unable to get out either. During the 1966-1967 school year, most of my friends were able to avoid the draft by staying in school, but other kids could not. Some, like Willy, became conscientious objectors. Willy felt so strongly anti-war that he got a mail-order theology degree and became the minister of his own church. With those credentials, he managed to avoid Vietnam also.

The police started getting antagonistic with the students, so we began to protest "the pigs" also. The situation on campus got very unstable. The situation was spreading from campus to campus across the nation.

More and more the protests made sense to me and I was sure of my role in the protests – that is, to support them wholeheartedly. Even though I would not normally have been drawn into something like that, the war was going nowhere, the world needed to change, and I was determined to be a part of the change. Just meeting boys and having fun was no longer enough for me. I needed to change the world. I could no longer sit by the sidelines and let the world go by.

Spring Break in Fort Lauderdale

In the Spring of 1967, my roommate Peggy found out about a really cheap trip to Fort Lauderdale for Spring break. Some UW students were chartering a bus and reserving group rooms. Peggy really pressed me into going. It was hard on my budget, but cheap enough that she talked me into it.

We set out one cold, dark Thursday evening. The bus left at six p.m. It was a busload of sixty partying college students with lots of beer. By dawn, we hit our half hour breakfast stop in Nashville, Tennessee, "home of 1352 guitar pickers," as the bus driver announced, based on the line from the popular song by the Lovin' Spoonful. We were tired and hung-over, but still excited about the trip. After a chance to wash our faces, brush our teeth, and have a bite of breakfast, we were back on the bus, excited again.

The early morning drive through the Smoky Mountains was spectacular. A silvery gray mist hung on the peaks, and we realized why they were called the Smokies. By mid-afternoon, we were in Chattanooga. The ice in our coolers had melted by then and several kids got off the bus to buy some. They came back, laughing.

"The people here don't even know what "ice" is," one of them said.

"Huh?" we asked.

"Well, we asked for ice and they just looked blank and said "what?" I said, "You know, that cold stuff you put in soda to cool it.""

"Oh, ii…ii…es," they said. Guess we're really in the south now."

Most of us had never been in the south and the accents were hard to catch. I think accents were more pronounced back then than they are now, after so many generations of television influence.

We arrived in Fort Lauderdale early Saturday morning, tired and ready to crash, but there were problems. Fourteen of us were dropped at one motel. It turned out that the desk clerk who made the reservations ran off with not only the money, but the registration book also. They had no idea who was coming. They didn't have room for all of us that night. They suggested that we store our stuff in their luggage room, change in the bathroom, and go to the beach for a few hours while they found space for all of us, which we did.

Before that trip, I was under the impression that my skin was dark enough not to get a major sunburn. Well, that may have been true in Wisconsin, but after three hours in the midday sun in south Florida in a two-piece bathing suit, I knew it wasn't true in Florida.

When Peggy and I went back to the motel to find out about accommodations, everyone looked at us and said, "Ouch!"

"It won't be bad," I kept insisting.

They didn't have room for us that night, so they sent us in cabs to the downtown Fort Lauderdale Holiday Inn for the night. They said to come back the next day, when they would have two suites available, one for the guys, one for the girls. Moving downtown sounded disruptive, but what could we do?

Once we checked in, we walked back to the beach area. We met a couple of guys and had a few drinks in their car in a parking lot. It was a pretty wild scene, lots of drinking. By the time we got back to our rooms, my sunburn was really hurting. Peggy felt pretty bad also.

The next morning, we went back to the original motel. Sure enough, they had space for us. The seven of us girls moved into a three-room suite. It had two double beds in the bedroom and sofa beds in the living room. We flipped a coin for rooms and Peggy and I ended up in the living room. Across the hall was a similar suite for the guys. Some of the other girls, who we didn't know before, were dating some of the guys, so they introduced us. We all became one big group that week.

My sunburn was still pretty bad. That's when one of the guys introduced me to Solarcaine ointment. Man, did that help!

The next night, several of us went down to one of the "in" bars. They were carding absolutely everyone. I almost made it in on my Wisconsin ID, but they noticed at the last second that I wasn't quite twenty-one and kicked me out. I told Peggy to go ahead and to meet me on a certain street corner in about an hour.

Before the hour was up, I was standing on the designated corner, waiting for Peggy, when a policeman came by.

"You can't stand here," he said. "Move it."

"I'm waiting for my friend," I said, innocently.

"Can't wait here!"

"But, how will I find my friend?" I pleaded.

"Move on," he said again. Then, when I still didn't move, he hit me sharply on the upper arm with his Billy club. I ran away in pain. I couldn't believe he would be so aggressive. It turns out there was an ordinance for Spring Break I hadn't heard about. Students were not allowed to loiter on street corners. After hours of roaming the streets, looking, I finally met up with Peggy. She had been roaming the streets, looking for me. We commiserated over what happened, then chocked it up to experience and went to dinner before all the restaurants closed. But, we did warn the others not to congregate on street corners.

Peggy and I were getting pretty low on money by mid-week. We had one meal a day paid for as part of our package. We used it for dinner, and pocketed the extra rolls and ate them for breakfast. But we were down to $4 and needed money for lunch when I had a great idea.

"Let's go to the grocery store and get hot dogs and buns."

We did. When we got back to the suite, two of the other girls and their boyfriends were there. When we started to cook hot dogs, one of the guys asked, "How much do you want for a hot dog? I'm hungry."

"50 cents," I replied.

We sold the extra six hot dogs for $3, so we had almost as much money as we started with. This worked out well. We ate the rest of the week, sold the extra, and still had money to make sandwiches for the trip home.

One day, when I returned to the apartment, I asked Peggy, "Do I need a haircut or something?"

"No, why?"

"Because the guys across the hall have started calling me "Mutt"."

"That's strange. Even more weird, they're calling me "Jeff"."

"Mutt 'n Jeff!" I exclaimed. "That solves it, only a joke, playing on our heights." Peggy was five feet ten and I was five feet zero.

We stopped being uptight and went out on the beach for a walk. Fort Lauderdale has vast stretches of white sand beaches, which are what draws so many people to the area in the first place. Peggy and I would walk several miles along the beach each morning. We walked barefoot, just where the waves lapped against our calves and then went back out again. I had never been to the ocean before, so I enjoyed it immensely. We would stop and collect seashells as we walked. Thousands of them were washed up on the shore by the tides -- sun-bleached white, and smoothed by the sand and surf. I marveled at all the people who did not seem to relish this natural environment. Most seemed to be paying attention to the people only, and ignoring this brush with nature. It was sad to me.

That particular day, I noticed what appeared to be some old balloons, washed up on shore by the last tide. I was just about to pick one up, when Peggy yelled, "Don't touch those!"

"Why? They're just old balloons."

"No, they're not. They're a type of jellyfish called a man-of-war, and they are poisonous. They can paralyze your limbs on contact."

Indelible Memories

Peggy and her family had been to the ocean before, so she knew about such things. I drew back my hand in disbelief of how such an innocent looking object could be so dangerous. By that afternoon, the beach patrol had placed signs on the beach, warning people about the danger of the men-of-war.

The last night of the trip, the guys across the hall had a big party. They invited all of us girls plus pretty much everyone they met all week. I was going to the party with a guy I met earlier in the week. He was a big guy, about 6'4" and 250 pounds, which was huge compared to my 5'0' and 115 pounds. He said he played football for the University of Illinois, although I wasn't quite sure I believed him.

He came over a little late, carrying a can of beer, which he opened and began drinking. He seemed a little drunk. The other girls had already gone across the hall to the party, so we were alone in the apartment. He kissed me. I didn't mind. In fact, I liked it. Then, his hands were all over me. I knew he wanted to go farther. I got scared and didn't know what to do. I didn't want to go any farther.

Then I saw the can of beer that he had put down on the coffee table. I grabbed the can of beer and poured it over his head and started laughing. He laughed too. We decided to go next door and join the party. I was glad it had gone no farther. I wasn't ready for more.

The next day we headed back to Wisconsin on the bus. I never saw him again. When I got back to the dorm, I remembered that a girl down the hall named Jen had gone to the University of Illinois the year before. I inquired about whether he really was an Illinois football player. She recognized the name and pulled out an Illinois football program.

"That him?" she asked, pointing to one of their first string players.

"Sure is!"

"He's a big star at Illinois. Did you meet him?"

"Yes, I met him in Fort Lauderdale. I poured a can of beer over his head for getting too fresh. Oh, well!"

It might have been nice to date a football player, but I was just glad to be back in Wisconsin dating Mike, when he was in town, and trying to get rid of Bill. The trip had been fun and a great learning experience, but I was missing the safety of a known environment.

Race Riots in Milwaukee

I saw my regular college friends rarely during the summer of 1967 when I stayed for summer school, except for my old roommate Peggy, and boyfriend Mike, who came to Madison for my twenty-first birthday in July. We had an elegant dinner at the Simon House, the best restaurant in town at the time. We had a great time and I missed them both. Thus, I was excited to get an invite to a party in Milwaukee in early August. It was at the Continental Motel, which seemed safe enough at the time. It was owned by Rick of the Baroque rock band's mother. Mike knew all of the band members well and we had all met them when they played in Madison. Mike grew up in Milwaukee's inner city on Thirteenth Street.

The Continental was a small motel on 30th Street and Wisconsin Avenue, on the main drag coming into Milwaukee. It was about a mile and a half from Mike's house and he worked there part-time that summer as a desk clerk.

The occasion for the party was Rick's birthday. We all came on Saturday afternoon. I came on the Badger Bus Line from Madison. Peggy came in her Mom's car. Mike walked and brought a friend named Jerry. All of the Baroques and the rest of the Continental staff were there too. We partied until the wee hours of the morning, dancing, drinking, singing, and talking. We then spent the night in a few unoccupied rooms and continued the fun on Sunday. We had all intended to leave Sunday evening. I had planned to take a return bus to Madison.

Peggy and I were still talking well into the evening. Mike's friend Jerry had made a big hit with Peggy. She repeated to me everything he had said to her at the party. She seemed very unsure of herself.

"Yes, it does sound like he's interested," I assured her.

"What should I do?"

"Just wait, he'll call you. He's got your number."

"I hope so."

This went on for hours. Later, she flipped channels on the TV and noticed that "Mutiny on the Bounty" was on. It was her favorite movie. She was so excited that she talked me into missing my bus to watch with her. When it was over, she drove home to West Bend. I asked Dan, who was working the front desk that night, to wake me at five a.m. so I could get the six o'clock bus and still catch my eight o'clock class.

When Dan called at five, he said, "Good morning, Carol. This is your wake-up call, but I'd recommend staying in bed, 'cause you're not getting out of town today."

"Why not?"

"Busses aren't running due to the race riots that erupted last night. The National Guard has the city cordoned off."

"Yeah, right! That's very funny, Dan"

"Put on the radio if you don't believe me. Never mind, no electricity! Better put on some clothes and come down here and listen with me on my portable."

I was scared then, but still not quite sure he wasn't joking, although the electricity really was off. I threw on some jeans and a t-shirt and went down to the lobby.

Indelible Memories

Sure enough, the city was in shambles. All roads in and out of the city were closed. The power was off citywide. A curfew was in effect for the entire city that prohibited all movement, including shopping and deliveries until further notice.

Mrs. B, Rick's mother, who owned the motel, came into the lobby about 5:30. She had just heard the news on her portable radio. She was surprised to see me, but was glad when I asked if I could help.

She enlisted me to help with the restaurant. She had enough emergency power to run some lights and to keep the refrigerators cool, but we were all glad when the power came back on about seven as it gave us additional options, like toast.

I became the waitress and toast maker. Mrs. B was the maitre d' and coffee maker. As the guests of the motel awakened to face the tough situation, we could at least seat them for breakfast and offer them coffee, cold cereal, and toast with jelly. Mrs. B offered it gratis. We explained that none of the staff could make it in due to the curfew, so we were unable to run the grill or to get more supplies.

Some of the guests grumbled that we couldn't serve eggs, but most were just glad that we were open and they could get their morning coffee. This was long before the days of coffee pots in motel rooms. Many of them were not aware of the riots before they entered the restaurant and my explanation was the first they heard. From my experience in Madison, I was conditioned to riots, but most of them were not. Many came from small Wisconsin towns, where they were isolated from such events.

"How long will this curfew last?" I got this question over and over.

"We don't know," was all I could answer. "Depends on when the National Guard gets things quieted down."

"Are we in any danger?"

"Not in the motel." I was sure of that at the time, anyway.

The different patrons had diverse opinions of the riots and some amount of arguing ensued. A lot of them wished that "those n____rs would keep themselves in their proper place." Personally, I was on the side of the blacks, based on how they were treated, but I kept my mouth shut about that at the time. I was staff of the motel, for the day, anyway. As such, I didn't want to heat up the argument lest I cause a riot myself.

As the day wore on, the situation got little better. I tried to call my roommates back in Madison to let them know I was OK, but was unable to get through. All telephone trunks were busy or reserved for emergency personnel. I thanked God I had not told my dad and stepmother where I was going — they thought I was safe in Madison.

When we went back to her room after lunch, Mrs. B worried out loud about her son Rick, who had gone to a party downtown the night before. He had not returned or called. "I hope he was lying in some girl's arms, and not rioting on the streets last night," she lamented to me.

"That's probably right," I replied. "Besides, he's probably trying to call and unable to get through." I recounted my experience trying to call my roommates in Madison. That calmed her down a little.

Mike returned to the motel in the late afternoon. I was glad to see him – Mrs. B was getting to be a bit of a pain in the neck about both Rick and the situation. She was worried that her dry cleaning would not be delivered of all things. They lifted the curfew for two hours so people could get necessary supplies. We sent Mike for extra bread, cold cuts, and milk so we could continue to offer a limited menu in the restaurant, and feed ourselves.

When darkness came, we began to hear the sound of gunshots, followed by police and fire sirens, in the distance. Worriedly, we huddled in Mrs. B's room. Her room was on the lower level, partially underground. We could see Wisconsin Avenue to the north, and had a partial view to the west through two sets of narrow windows at eye level. We sent Mike to the lobby to look east.

Mike came back screaming, "They just set fire to the Holiday Inn!" The Holiday Inn was on the next block east of us. "Lots of rioters on the street," he continued.

We heard shouts outdoors and began to plan our escape should they set fire to our building (or worse!). Dan would sound the fire alarm and we would lead an evacuation out the back door. I hadn't been this scared since lying on the floor by the lockers with my hands over my head during the Cuban Missile Crisis in 1962! I thought about the people I had reassured in the morning about their safety in the motel. I had no idea in the morning that this could happen.

Luckily, the police, aided by the National Guard, held the line before it got to the Continental, so we were spared an evacuation. The National Guard recommended blackout procedures at night for all the motels and hotels in the area. We began to put them into practice. A lot of the patrons were visibly scared, but were unable to go anywhere else, so they had to tolerate the situation. The curfew was finally lifted on Tuesday afternoon. Rick came over to comfort his mother. Yes, he had been in his girlfriend's arms, not in the riots. I was able to get the Badger Bus Line back to Madison on Wednesday morning, to the joy of my worried roommates.

Mike wrote me a letter the following week. The motel continued the blackout procedures until the following Sunday, but no further incidents occurred, except for a single gunshot on the corner of 30th and Michigan, in front of the church. And, yes, Peggy and Jerry were seeing each other. I was relieved.

Murder on Campus

During spring semester, 1968, I was taking two computer courses and both of them had programs that needed to be written and debugged. In those days, computer programs were punched on cards and entered into the computer via a card reader. After submitting the cards at the computing desk, one had to wait for the program to be queued and run. After hours, sometimes days, the program would run and a computer printout on fanfold paper would be delivered back to the computing desk with the results – a very time-consuming process. On top of that, the computers for each of my courses were in separate buildings. One was in the computer science building, one in Sterling Hall, the physics building.

A friend gave me a tip that the computer in Sterling Hall wasn't as busy on Sunday, so you could get a turnaround time of only an hour or so. One cold, wet May Sunday, I spent the day walking between Sterling Hall and the computer science building, submitting card decks at both, and looking at the results as soon as they came in. I would then make appropriate upgrades and resubmit them. I must have been in and out of Sterling Hall at least six times that day.

The next day in class, a friend asked me, "Did you hear about the murder on campus yesterday?"

"No, where?"

"They don't know where the murder took place, but they found the body of the young girl outside of Sterling Hall." [Yes, this is the same Sterling Hall physics building that was bombed in August of 1970.]

"Where?"

"In the bushes by the stairs."

"Oh my God! I was in and out of Sterling Hall all day yesterday, running and debugging my computer program. I went up and down those stairs at least six times. What time did it happen?"

"They think it happened in the morning when the girl was jogging. But a student found the body last night."

"You mean I walked by that body about six times?"

"Sounds that way."

"Was she a student?"

"Yeah, a freshman."

"Do they know who did it?"

"No, no idea. They're investigating."

As we finished the year, we were all scared. We had all felt safe on the campus. Most of us even hitchhiked rides across campus; at least we did before that incident. Afterward, we tried to move in groups as much as possible. The investigation continued, we heard about it often in *The Daily Cardinal*, the campus newspaper, but they never did find out who did it.

**Grandma and the "old coot" at my sister's wedding in
1955**

That Old Coot?

[The Last Time I Saw Grandma]

Aunt Edith stopped by our house in New Richmond
one wintry December day in the late 1960's. She knew I was

home from college and thought I might want to see my grandparents. I did.

My mother's parents had moved off of the farm in the early 1950's and retired to a cozy two-story home in the nearby tiny town of Somerset, Wisconsin. They were high on the hill, across from St. Anne's Catholic Church. It was a comfortable home, but with no modern amenities. Grandpa didn't want them. He rose at 4:30 every morning to go outdoors to get wood to put in the cookstove so it would be hot by the time Grandma cooked breakfast. He claimed it was good for him. It was. Grandpa never spent a day in the hospital until he was eighty and his appendix got infected.

Grandma had birthed fourteen children. Eleven of them survived to adulthood and had kids of their own. Grandma knitted a pair of mittens each year for each grandchild for the first forty. After that, she turned to store-bought gifts. Her mittens were tighter woven and warmer than any store-bought ones ever. I can attest to that myself.

When Aunt Edith and I arrived, Grandma was sitting on an old wooden chair in her ancient kitchen, yelling at Grandpa. It wasn't a special occasion, just a regular weekday afternoon. Grandma's long gray hair was pushed up with combs like she always wore it. She wore a cotton print housedress and those black lace-up shoes with the two-inch heels that old ladies always wore back then. She smiled when she saw me.

"Leona," she yelled. "Good to see you."

"No, no, Gram. This is Carol Jean, Leona's daughter," Aunt Edith said.

"No, it's Leona," Grandma insisted.

My mother had died about ten years earlier. I had no idea what to say. Luckily, Aunt Edith was a big talker. She

163

went on about the bad drive over, through the snow, while I took my coat off and hung it on the back of a chair.

I hadn't realized until that moment that Grandma had alzheimers disease, in today's parlance. We called it hardening of the arteries back then.

Grandma called me Leona again to get my attention. Grandpa was sitting in the far corner of the room, wearing dark woolen trousers and a heavy flannel shirt, and puffing on his pipe. He'd had enough. "Not Leona, Ma. It's Carol Jean!" he yelled.

Grandma looked at him, and then looked at Aunt Edith, and asked, "Who's that old coot?"

"Why, that's your husband, John," my aunt answered.

"Nah, my John's a handsome young man, not an old coot like that."

My jaw dropped. I turned to look at Grandpa, expecting anger, but he was laughing his head off.

We made small talk, ate Christmas cookies, and ignored Grandma's foibles. When the early dusk of December began to steal the light, Aunt Edith drove me back home. I was glad I went. It was the last time I ever saw Grandma.

Mousie in the kitchen

My dad parked himself in the corner of the kitchen, by the low, makeshift counter, created when he raised the top of the ancient wooden cabinet a couple of feet off its base with boards. He sat on a chrome kitchen chair with a yellow vinyl seat, a Winston cigarette dangling from the corner of his lip. A carton of Winstons, as always, stood sideways on the counter behind him, next to the ceramic cookie jar topped with a sombrero. It was his usual perch when he came out to the kitchen to be sociable.

He was in his late forties and already a grandfather several times over. A handsome man in his youth, he was balding and developing a beer belly. His hair was combed straight back to cover his bald spot, but this was no longer working, since there were so few hairs, they separated into strands. He always wore a hat outdoors, to protect his balding head from sunburn. This gave him a tan line across his brow — white forehead above, ruddy tan face below. Heavy black plastic bifocals were balanced on his large-pored nose.

I was standing by the sink, washing green-leaf lettuce for the salad, shaking it dry and putting it in the heavy beige bowl with the single brown stripe around the top that we always used for salad. His first three grandchildren, my sister Lucy's kids, were visiting. Ricky, who was about five at the time, came running from the dining room, in between my dad and me, with an old metal airplane in his hand. He was mouthing an engine noise, "Zum-zum."

As he passed, my dad grabbed him around the waist.

"Tut, tut, tut," he clucked his tongue. "Hold still a second."

"But I'm flying," Ricky said, protesting.

A few tickles in the ribs made Ricky giggle so hard he had to stop. My dad pointed his index finger at the other side of the kitchen, behind the gray Formica-topped chrome table, to the thickly painted willow-green wainscoting. My eyes followed the finger, as did Ricky's.

"Ricky! See that round hole in the woodwork over there, behind the table?"

"Ya."

"You just watch. That's where the mousie comes out."

Ricky stared at the spot for the longest time.

"There's no mousie," he said.

"Is too. You just watch."

"I'll get my sister."

He went into the dining room and soon came back with two and a half year old Linda toddling behind him.

"Linny, watch," he said, pointing to the hole in the wainscoting, "A mousie's gonna come out of there."

"Mousie?"

Soon Linda was staring at the hole with him, wide-eyed with expectation. My sister Lucy snuck up behind them.

"Whatcha doing kids?" she asked.

"Waiting for the mousie to come out of that hole."

"There's no mousie in that hole."

"Grandpa said so."

"You just watch out, or that mousie will get you," my dad laughed.

The kids stared quietly at the hole every time they visited for years. They never did see the mousie that my dad and I reported seeing often when they weren't looking.

The Telepherique De L'Aiguille Du Midi

Crossing from France into Italy in a Cable-car

From the first morning of the trip, when we skied a double-black diamond trail by mistake (jetlag?), to the day Mitch fell and hit his head with a ski and got amnesia, to the day the crevice showed up on the off-piste trail we'd been skiing every day, I didn't think my fear could get much worse.

But after we skied the Vallee Blanche glacier, twelve miles from top to bottom, we looked for more. During some après ski with our guide on the Vallee Blanche, he mentioned that one could take a gondola from the Aiguille Du Midi, high on Mont Blanc, to a spot on an Italian peak and ski into

168

Courmeyeur, but only with a guide. We asked if he could take us, and he said, "Of course."

Back at the hotel that evening, we recruited several more men from our tour group to join us, but no other women were interested. But, when we told our female tour guide on the trip, Helena from Denmark, she volunteered to join us. But, she knew a guide named Dominic, who was an expert guide for the trip. She insisted on arranging it with him. It was a go.

Mitch and I had been skiing daily with a man named Nigel. His wife, Allie, had fallen and wrenched her knee the first day and limped in a bulky cast the rest of the trip. Nigel, Mitch, and I all wore navy blue pants and yellow jackets. We followed each other in a line, looking like a ski team.

Allie joined us the morning of the excursion into Italy. She wanted to take the gondola over and back. She limped

Telecabine Panoramique Mont Blanc

along with us as we walked almost a mile in ski boots across the town of Chamonix at 8:30 that morning. We went to the base of the Telepherique De L'Aiguille Du Midi, which would take us to the top of the Aiguille Du Midi in a 72 passenger car, 3842 meters from a base of 1035 meters, which is about 9000 feet. The elevation change was too much to span with one cable, so we changed to another car at Plan De L'Aiguille, 2317 meters.

At the top, we drank hot cocoa and rested for about twenty minutes to acclimate to the severe altitude change. Then, the four of us got into the small gondola named Telecabine Panoramique Mont Blanc, which took us from the Aiguille Du Midi to Punta Helbronner, an Italian peak, a distance of 5093 meters.

Allie took lots of photos and said she "enjoyed her trip," when we disembarked into a hewn rock in the peak. She stayed on the car for the trip back.

We had been told to bring our passports "just in case" and it was fortunate we did because way up there, at 11,371 feet, in the hewn rock landing was an Italian Customs Agent in a rock office with an open window, calling out, "Passports please." He stamped each of our passports and we walked through the rest of the "cave" and back out into the crisp sunny day.

Dominic explained that we needed to follow a trail around the peak to another trail on the other side. We attached our skis and began following him. I was only 28 years old at the time, but, at that altitude, I was soon puffing like the big bad wolf. I had to stop several times to get my breath. Soon, I was at the back of the line, struggling to keep sight of them. The trail went about a half mile and ended where a packed ski trail was carved into the side of the mountain. Ropes were tied to stakes pummeled into the slope. The rope was to be used as a handhold if necessary. Dominic led the group around a curve and Helena followed behind him instead of bringing up the rear as I thought she should.

As the men rounded the curve one by one, they each turned and looked back at me, looking me over top to bottom, and then shaking their heads, "no." I shrugged, wondering, but kept inching forward as the group progressed.

When I rounded the curve, I gasped. Just ahead, the carved trail had slipped loose due to the elements or too many skiers. I didn't know why, but I watched as one of the men grabbed the rope and slid past the loosened part of the trail. Then, I realized why they were looking back at me. I was too short to reach the trail if I grabbed the rope! A whirlwind of ideas flashed through my mind. Should I turn around and go back alone? Should I trust my skis on the sliding loose part of the trail without the rope? I wasn't sure I could do either. Luckily, my adrenaline was rushing.

When it was my turn, I grasped the rope and slid forward. As the slope slid away, I was hanging from the rope with my hands. I looked down. The slope was so steep I thought I would die for sure if I fell. I knew I couldn't hang on forever. I braved it and let go with my left hand and moved it forward, grabbing the rope again. My body moved forward with it. Next, I let go with my right hand and moved it forward. My muscles ached, but I managed to hand over hand it on the rope for the four feet or so when my skis didn't touch the ground.

When they finally touched again, I was shaking all over. I moved slowly to the end of the hewn trail and then traversed forward slowly to the slope below where I could make a turn. On the slope, I collapsed in a heap and tried to catch my breath.

"This will help," I heard a voice from above me.

I looked up. Donald, an English gentleman with our tour group, held a bottle of sunscreen and handed it toward me.

"That's not going to help," I said.

"It's not what you think," Donald said. "Open it and pour a capful."

I took the bottle and opened it, smelling the distinct odor of brandy.

"Aha," I said. I shakily poured a capful and chugged it. The warmth of the drink pulsed through my body and my shaking began to subside.

"Have another," Donald said.

I did. It was a small cap.

"Thank you," I said. "I think you just saved my day."

Dominic signaled us to start down the slope to Courmayeur. I managed to stand on my skis and start down. Another guy named Mike and I brought up the rear. The whole group skied down the manageable run for twenty minutes or so. Then, Dominic stopped and told Helena something.

"He says you're going too slowly. You won't be able to do this slope twice at this rate," Helena said.

Twice! I thought. *Once was bad enough.*

But the guys all nodded and we continued down. With relief, I noted that everyone was skiing *slower*. I loved the slope and got a kick out of skiing through a tunnel near the bottom. We made it to Courmayeur. Helena found us an outdoor table at a restaurant in town. It was nice and warm down there.

This was Italy! They know how to do lunch with finesse. Four courses and almost three hours later, Dominic had Helena mention that "He thought you wanted to ski Courmayeur today. You have to do it now if you want to get some runs before closing."

We all got tickets and went up the chairlift. Dominic gave us a few options. Most went for some black diamond slopes, but Mike and I opted for a slow snowplow down a catwalk. We said we would meet them at the bottom.

It was warm and the snow was slushy. Mike and I made it to the bottom where we saw Dominic and the others waiting at the edge of a river. I looked for a bridge, but didn't see one. Then, I noticed the flat-rock stepping stones crossing the river.

In ski boots? I thought. *Carrying skis?* I was too exhausted to cope.

Dominic saw my reluctance and volunteered to carry my skis. I accepted and followed him across. I felt just a little bit bad when Dominic stepped into the shallow water that went over his ski boots. He was not happy.

We made it across, where Jean-Pierre from our hotel met us with the van and delivered us through the thirteen-mile Chamonix tunnel and back into town. Helena rode off with Dominic when we arrived.

Aha, that's why she insisted on Dominic, I thought.

Run for the Tree

Dave and I moved into our first (and only) house in Lisle, Illinois in 1977. We loved the openness of the contemporary home in the brand-new suburb called Green Trails, but mostly we loved the setting on a wooded lot that backed up on a park, complete with a playground and a tennis court.

We installed a cement-block patio off of the sliding-glass door in our family room and enjoyed watching the squirrels scamper from tree to tree. Mostly, we enjoyed the gnarly old oak in the far corner of the patio. A hole in the trunk, just above the bottom branch, housed families of squirrels each Spring.

We had only lived there about a year and a half when one large branch that jutted out at an angle over the scruffy yard (grass doesn't grow well on a wooded lot), failed to produce leaves and needed to be removed for the health of the tree and the safety of us and our visitors. Dave, always the do-it-yourselfer, carried his shiny new aluminum extension ladder out of the garage and leaned it against the tree. He spent most of the morning throwing yellow plastic ropes over the branch, "so you can pull it away from the tree when I cut it with a saw."

I was young, petite, and skeptical. "Me?' I asked.

"Yes, you. Just pull the rope when I tell you to."

I stood in the middle of the yard and surveyed the situation, while Dave climbed the ladder with our yellow electric chain saw. "That branch is going to come down and hit the ladder you're standing on!" I yelled.

"Nah!" he said. "Just grab that rope and run for the tree."

Now, I'm in the middle of the wooded lot, surrounded by trees, and half-deaf Dave is starting to saw.

"Which tree?" I yelled at a volume I heretofore had never been able to reach.

"Over there," he motioned with his head and continued sawing.

I ran with the rope, pulling as I ran. The cut end of the branch fell straight down as it separated from the tree and, just as I predicted, swung down and slammed into a rung of the ladder that Dave was standing on. The sharp screech of the buckling aluminum was louder than the blue words Dave yelled as the ladder wobbled under him and the chainsaw swung wildly in his right hand as his left held tight to the top rung of the ladder.

I expected the whole thing to crash to the ground, Dave included, but after what seemed like an eternity, the swaying stopped. The branch hung against the dented rung, the top part stuck on another limb. The other end hung over a branch of a tree on the other side of the yard. I kept pulling on the attached rope, but it won't budge.

"What do I do now?" I asked.

"Pull the branch out of the way!"

"I can't," I yelled, 'it's stuck."

175

Dave's knees were still shaking. He held tight to the ladder. "Carefully let go of the rope and come and grab the chain saw," he said, more calmly that I expected.

As I eased up on the rope, the branch settled into the ladder but didn't knock it over. I let go and reached up for the saw and carefully set it on the grass.

Dave managed to step down the ladder in between some twigs, past the main shaft of the branch, and onto *terra firma*.

"Whew, that was close!" he said.

"I told ya it was gonna hit the ladder," I reminded him.

"Ya, you did." He shook his head.

"How are we gonna unstick the branch?" I asked.

"Just get out of the way while I pull the ladder out," he said.

He pulled the twigs out of the rungs and then pulled the ladder out from behind the branch. The branch still hung there, caught on a branch above. He tied yet another rope on the branch. "Ok," he said, "if we both pull hard, I think we can free it."

"We'll probably break the other branch," I said. We both pulled and the branch came free, not without cracking the other branch and bending the branch of the other tree down over the yard.

The ladder seemed to be ok, despite the large welt in one rung, so Dave went back up and cut off the cracked branch.

The branches Dave removed created a little more light and gave us the opportunity to try a garden on our small wooded lot. We tried! The tomato plants grew seven feet high as they looked for sunshine. Only a few tiny tomatoes ripened on the vines. The carrots and lettuce fared better than the scraggly green-pepper plants. As soon as the tree grew more branches, we gave up on the whole thing.

The tree lasted a few more years. We watched the baby squirrels each year as they emerged from their tree-hole and learned to climb on the branches. And then, one year, the leaves failed to emerge and Dave used the same dented aluminum extension ladder to take the tree down. He tied more ropes to the top for me to pull and made his first cut through the trunk just above the squirrel hole. We managed to drop the top without hitting the ladder. I was cheering when Dave yelled, "Oh, noooo!"

"What now?" I yelled.

He pointed into the hollow tree. "Baby squirrels!" he yelled back. "What do we do now?"

"If we leave them alone," I said, "the mother may come back for them."

We went inside and watched from the family room window. Mama squirrel must have been watching because it was only a few minutes before she climbed up the tree trunk and emerged from the hole with the nape of the neck of the first tiny squirrel firmly in her jaws. She carried it carefully across the yard and into the woods beyond. A few minutes later, she came back for her next baby. She did that four times. We waited a long time to make sure she was done before we finished the tree removal.

We missed watching the babies that year, but we were glad to know that they were safe in the woods.

Wisdom Teeth!

I was thirty and the gums far in back on the left side of my jaw hurt. I went to see my dentist. I stepped up the creaky stairs of the ancient building on Lisle Main Street. Doc Lenart was in his late sixties and in the last year of his practice, although neither of us knew that at the time.

After a quick exam, he declared, "You're teething!"

"What?" I asked. Teething was for babies and toddlers, not your local IBM representative.

"You heard me right," he said. "It's a wisdom tooth. I'd recommend Orajel."

"Don't you need to take it out?" Every wisdom tooth I ever heard of had been removed.

"Not necessarily," he said. "Sometimes they grow in fine."

I stopped at the drugstore to buy the tiny bottle of brownish liquid. I was sure the clerk thought it was for my newborn. It took care of the pain while the large tooth broke through the skin and then stopped. Nothing happened for another ten years. And then, just before my fortieth birthday, the pains can back. This time on both sides of my mouth.

By this time old Doc Lenart had passed away and I was seeing his replacement, young Dr. Gonda. He was in his brand new suite of offices on the other side of Main Street. One of his assistants led me back to her chair. X-rays were taken and developed on the spot.

"H'mm," Dr. Gonda stroked his chin as he stared at the full set of x-rays. "See," he pointed, "those wisdom teeth are infected. Got to come out!"

I cringed. "All of them? I asked.

"Yup."

He explained that he didn't pull teeth and referred me to an oral surgeon in nearby Naperville named Dr. Blecha. Little did I know how well I'd get to know him. It was supposed to be easy. He'd put me in something called "twilight sleep," remove all four impacted and infected teeth and I'd be on my way. I'd need to follow-up in a couple of weeks, just to make sure all was well.

I was still in 'twilight sleep" from the surgery when the Doc came out and gave instructions to me and my half deaf husband.

I went home with my teeth packed in gauze. I didn't realize it was packed with potent medicine until I sat on a deck chair on our patio that evening with a glass of wine. The glass went one way and I went the other as the wine took effect.

"But I didn't even take a pain pill yet," I said. My words slurred.

My husband shrugged his shoulders.

"Did you get some paper instructions this morning?" I asked.

"Yeah," he replied. "On the counter."

I stumbled in and read them. "Didn't he tell you about the medicine packed in my teeth?"

"You were there too," he said.

"In body only," I said. "What else did he say?"

"Somethin' about hitting a nerve. Might be some chips in there," he answered.

I didn't say more.

I'd scheduled the surgery on Friday so I could be back in the office to run the first important meeting of my first project on my new job. I could barely open my mouth but I went anyway. I mumbled my way through and called Doc Blecha. That afternoon, I began my every two day trek to get my mouth repacked. No steak! No wine! Only soup, yogurt, and milk. I was in misery.

The following Saturday, my husband tried to cheer me up by taking me on a sailing outing on our boat on Silver Lake. We headed up to Wisconsin early with our three year old son, Stevie. It was a calm morning and soon Stevie got bored and curled up in the small cutty-cabin of our fourteen foot O'Day Day Sailer and fell asleep.

I was sitting there in my misery, not opening my mouth, when the wind came up. The sail jibed and one of the lines got caught on the foredeck. My husband climbed up to loosen it. When he did, the sail moved fast toward the left side of my jaw!

"Grab the sheet, it's going over!" my husband yelled.

There was no way I was going to risk my sore jaw to "grab a sheet."

"No!" I screamed. "I can't!"

Then, I remembered innocent Stevie, asleep in a boat that was about to go over.

"Help!" was all I could manage as I dove under the sail. My husband did a flying leap off the foredeck and into the main cabin, pushing me down in the seat as he landed. He grabbed the sheet and the boat righted itself. Stevie rolled over and went back to sleep.

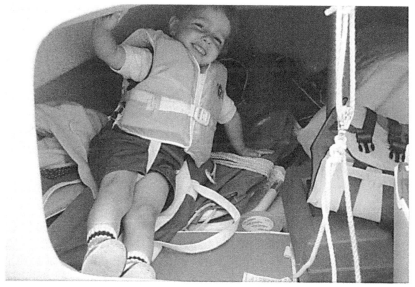

Stevie in the cutty-cabin

My husband relaxed a bit and looked at me. "You shoulda grabbed the sheet," he said.

I just pointed to my jaw. No way was I gonna open my mouth.

Two months later, my jaw finally healed and my treks to Blecha's office ended. The work project I had started on such a bad note never did go smoothly. There must be some lesson in this!

"By the Power of Stevie Daniel"

My son was three and a half and totally enamored with He-Man, the hero of the *Masters of the Universe* TV series. My husband's Aunt Dee, who wasn't actually his aunt, but his mother's best friend, had hooked our son on the series at the tender age of two when she gifted him with He-Man—his first action figure. Little did I understand what was behind the twinkle in her eyes as I said, "Thank-you."

Soon, our home was littered with the plastic figures with names that matched their personas—Skeletor, Buzz-Off, Moss Man, and Evil-Lyn. New ones came out every week and our local supermarket kept up with the stream in their toy department. Each figure came with a small comic-book story and a flyer of associated products that my son soon labeled, "All the rest you can get."

But the series didn't stop with the figures. Soon, there was He-Man's castle and his arch-rival Skeletor's Castle Grayskull. There were vehicles with battery-operated motors to take the figures to imaginary wars. Each figure came with a small weapon to throw or hit or spin. All had to be recovered from the carpet before the vacuum ate them up.

There were so many products, that we needed several huge boxes to store them in the attic when they lost their hold on our son, but seemed like they might be worth something one day. Years later, when we moved to Wisconsin, they came along and are now in our storage shed. Seems it's hard to get rid of a complete collection of this stuff.

He-Man's girlfriend was named Teela; Skeletor's was named Evil-Lyn. When our family sailboat needed a name, we explained that boats were usually given women's names. We still have a sailboat named Teela.

He-Man had a sword that lit up magically when he raised it high and gave him added strength, "By the power of He-Man". Soon, they were selling large plastic swords that lit up for little boys.

I resisted when he was two and a half and three. Being stabbed, even by plastic, was not my idea of responsible motherhood.

But then, one day when he was three and a half, we went to the county fair. It was July, hot and sticky in our Chicago suburb. My husband was in Pennsylvania, where his mother was hospitalized. After all the grim conversations about Grammie, I felt my son needed a treat.

He noticed the gift tent first. "Look at all the stuff you can get," he warned me.

"Not now," I said. "We'd have to carry it around all day."

We rode the Ferris wheel, the small roller-coaster, the Merry-Go-Round, and the flying airplanes. We pulled rubber duckies out of a river and won small trinkets. We shot rubber frogs into a lily-pond. We ate hotdogs, shared an elephant ear, and drank lemonade. My son even got to control a real crane (with the help of an operator).

We petted the calves, sheep and goats in one barn. We looked at bunnies, ducks, chickens and turkeys in another. We picked up hard candy and brochures, suckers and balloons at the endless series of booths. We were hot, sticky, dirty, and catsupy when I announced it was time to go home. My son agreed! I was amazed at the ease of our departure until we passed the gift tent on the way out.

"Now, I can get a toy," he announced and he ran into the tent.

"Huh?" I asked.

"You said we had to wait until the end so we didn't have to carry it all day."

Pretty good logic for a three year old, I thought. I was about to argue with him, but then, my blond little boy in bright red shorts and a white t-shirt stained with catsup, picked up a red plastic light-up sword, held it high in the air and said in a thundering voice, "By the power of Stevie Daniel!"

I caved in.

House Mouse

A few telltale droppings on the kitchen floor first alerted me of his presence. "We've got a mouse in the house!" I told my husband, Dave.

"I'll get some D-Con," he replied.

"Oh, don't kill the poor thing," my son Steve pleaded. "Maybe we can live-trap it." Steve was in junior high and a born savior of all of Earth's species, large and small.

Dave and Steve headed to the hardware store. They came back with small metal box-traps. We set small chunks of cheese on the inside levers. The lever was supposed to trip the door when the mouse nibbled the cheese, trapping him inside. We put a couple in the kitchen.

The next morning, there were more droppings. I peeked inside the traps. The cheese was gone, but doors were still open.

"Maybe we have to squish the cheese on there," I said. "You know, so it sticks."

But the next morning we still had open doors and no cheese.

"Let's try peanut butter," Steve said. "They couldn't just take it, they'd have to lick it."

Still no luck!

That night, I saw him for the first time. I was watching TV on our big brown chair with my feet up on the hassock.

Indelible Memories

The tiny gray creature hopped up the top basement step and ran past the front of the TV. He was almost to the hassock when he saw me staring and stopped cold. We stared at each other for almost a full minute, and then he ran between the hassock and the chair, right under my feet and into the kitchen.

"You brazen hunk of fur," I yelled after him. By the time I got to the kitchen, he was nowhere in sight.

The same thing happened the next night. The following morning, I found droppings up on the counter. This had to stop.

That evening, after work, I moved every object on the counter and looked behind it. I found droppings in the corner, behind Steve's forgotten Halloween pumpkin-bucket. Inside the bucket, I found a stale Hershey bar with a chewed wrapping and a sticky Dum-Dum. *Aha, so this was the attraction.* I threw the candy in the garbage, bucket and all.

That night, I watched the creature scurry under my feet and head for the kitchen. I followed quickly and caught him climbing up the phone cord that was trailing over the edge of the counter. *So that's how he got up there.*

We had a family conference and the consensus was to get a better trap, but still to catch it live. Dave and Steve came home with a trap that was big enough for a squirrel. Seemed like overkill.

"But the sensor closes the door as soon as he goes in there. Even if he doesn't eat the cheese," Dave explained.

We set it up, but the mouse wouldn't go in there. We saw him running around, but I think he was scared of the huge entrance.

Then one morning, Steve was coming down the stairs before school. The mouse was sitting on the floor, below the bottom step. When he looked up and saw Steve's foot coming down on him, he ran for his life so fast, he ran right into the trap.

Steve didn't want to let the mouse go free outdoors because there was snow out there, but Dave convinced him the creature would find shelter.

The next day after work, I parked the car in the garage and went down the driveway to get the mail. When I got back to the top of the driveway, I saw a small gray blob in the track my tire had made in the snow. When I got closer, I realized it was the small gray mouse, flattened thin and no longer breathing.

Revelations

It was the summer of 2004 and my sister Lucy and I were both getting past middle age. Lucy was 68 and I was 58. Lucy was visiting our Wisconsin vacation condo for Fourth of July as usual. I'd been forced into an early retirement. My husband Dave had too, but he was busy working at a boat store in Lombard, Illinois, so Lucy and I had lots of time for just the two of us.

We were at the condo pool one afternoon. The weather was clear and bright. The sun rays were sparkling on the crystal-blue water. I swam down to the shallow end of the pool after an underwater swim. Lucy didn't swim, but she was sitting on the edge of the cement deck, her feet dangling in the water. When I walked over, we chatted a bit about the full length memoir of my life up to age twenty-two that I had just finished. Drafted, actually, but I didn't know that yet.

She mentioned a couple of errors in the memoir. I had sent her husband to the wrong Army Reserve camp, no big deal, but the scene about Mumma holding her two-month-old daughter Lin in the hospital on Easter was definitely wrong. She had sorely wanted Mumma to hold Lin, but the nurses were adamantly against it. Lucy said that she supposed it was because of the staph infection.

"I remember that," I said. "They wouldn't let me even visit her anymore because there was a staph infection somewhere in that ward, I think."

"You don't know?" she said. "It was Mumma that had the staph."

"Phew!" The air whistled through my lips. "No wonder they wouldn't let me in!" I said. "It never made sense before."

We talked more about the memoir and how Mumma's death had affected both of our lives. She asked why I hadn't continued the memoir on to my adult life, especially the part about Michael.

I stammered and got defensive. Michael was my son who was born extremely premature in 1981, lived 23 days, and died. I couldn't write about it yet, even though it had been 23 years. I told Lucy that.

"But you did all you could to save him," she said.

That was true. When my water broke, I thought I was only 25 weeks along. My doctor said I was having a miscarriage when I got to the hospital, but I was not able to accept that. I asked if he was sure, since I wasn't in labor yet. He was young and said he would check with another doctor. When he came back, he packed me into an ambulance and sent me to Loyola University Hospital.

It was quite a ride. The male paramedic rode in back with me. His female partner drove because she "didn't do babies."

I lay for eight days in an inverted bed with my head lower than my middle, trying to stave off early labor, which didn't work. On the eighth day, I went into labor anyway. My white blood cell count was up that day, so they wouldn't give me drugs to stop the labor, thinking it better I deliver than pass on the infection. Michael was born at 4 a.m. on the ninth morning, actually a very small (one pound twelve ounce) 31 week baby, not 26 as we expected. They put him in the Neonatal Intensive Care Unit (NICU).

"I know," I told Lucy at the pool. "I tried. I had to. If I hadn't it would have been almost like an abortion to me. And you know how I feel about that."

"Yeah, I know," she said. "Somehow, you seem to have got that from Mumma, but you surely don't even know."

"Know what?" I asked.

"Well, you know that Mumma had cancer before you were born?"

"I know she had a hysterectomy when I was two. Was that the cancer?"

"It was, but did you know Mumma had that cancer when she was carrying you?"

My jaw dropped. "Oh my God, no!"

"The doctor wanted her to abort you. He was afraid you would be born a monster, but Mumma wouldn't do it."

If I hadn't been in the pool with a lot of other condo owners around, I would have screamed. I thought about what she said. I might not have *been* if Mumma had made the other decision.

"But what happened?" I asked.

"Mumma was right. I watched her check you over after you were born. She said, 'Ten fingers, ten toes. Looks fine except for the underbite.'"

We both laughed. "I still have the underbite," I said.

I'm glad Lucy told me. It hasn't changed my life but it has changed how I think about life.

Made in the USA
Monee, IL
01 October 2020

43723451R00115